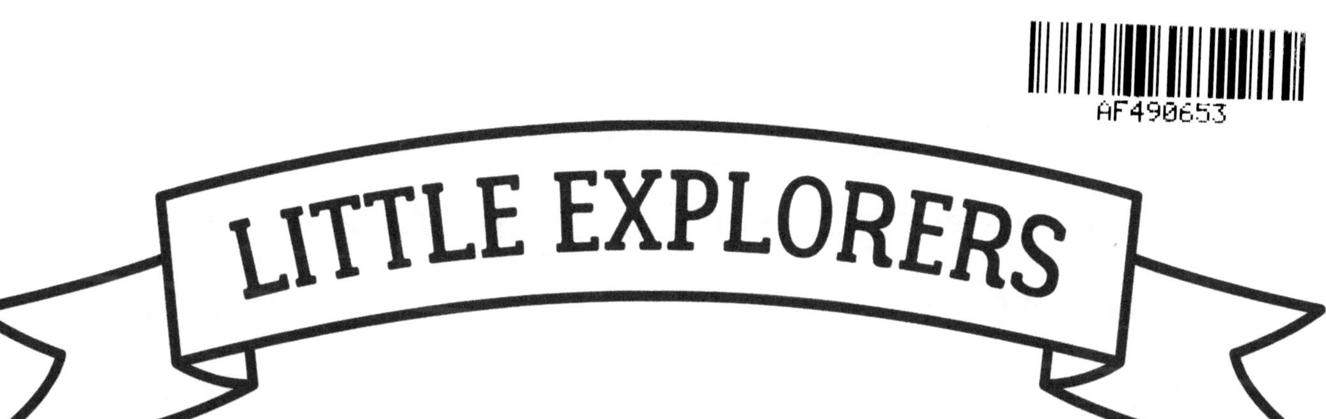

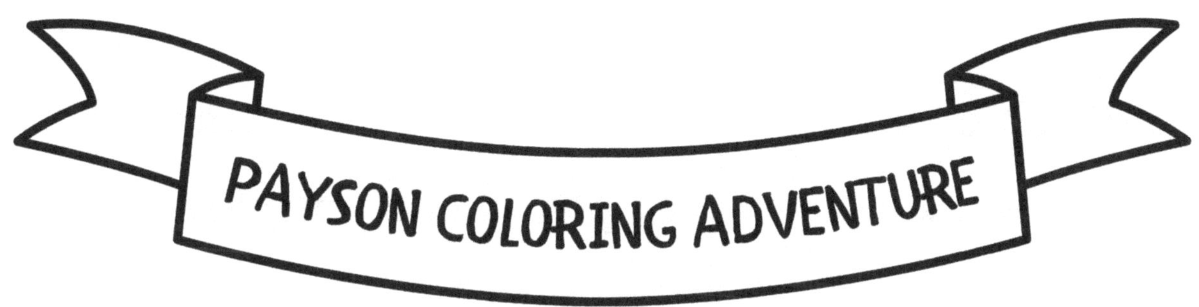

CREATED BY KATHERINE BLUMA

PUBLISHED BY MY SUCCESS STRATEGIST

**Welcome to Payson,
known as the heart of Arizona!**

This book is full of fun adventures and amazing places. You'll see cool spots like the Mogollon Rim and the Natural Bridge, meet animals like elk and insects, and think about fun activities like off-roading, hiking, and swimming.

Each page has a special question just for you to make your plans for your next adventure even more exciting.

**Question:
Are you ready to explore Payson
and have lots of fun?**

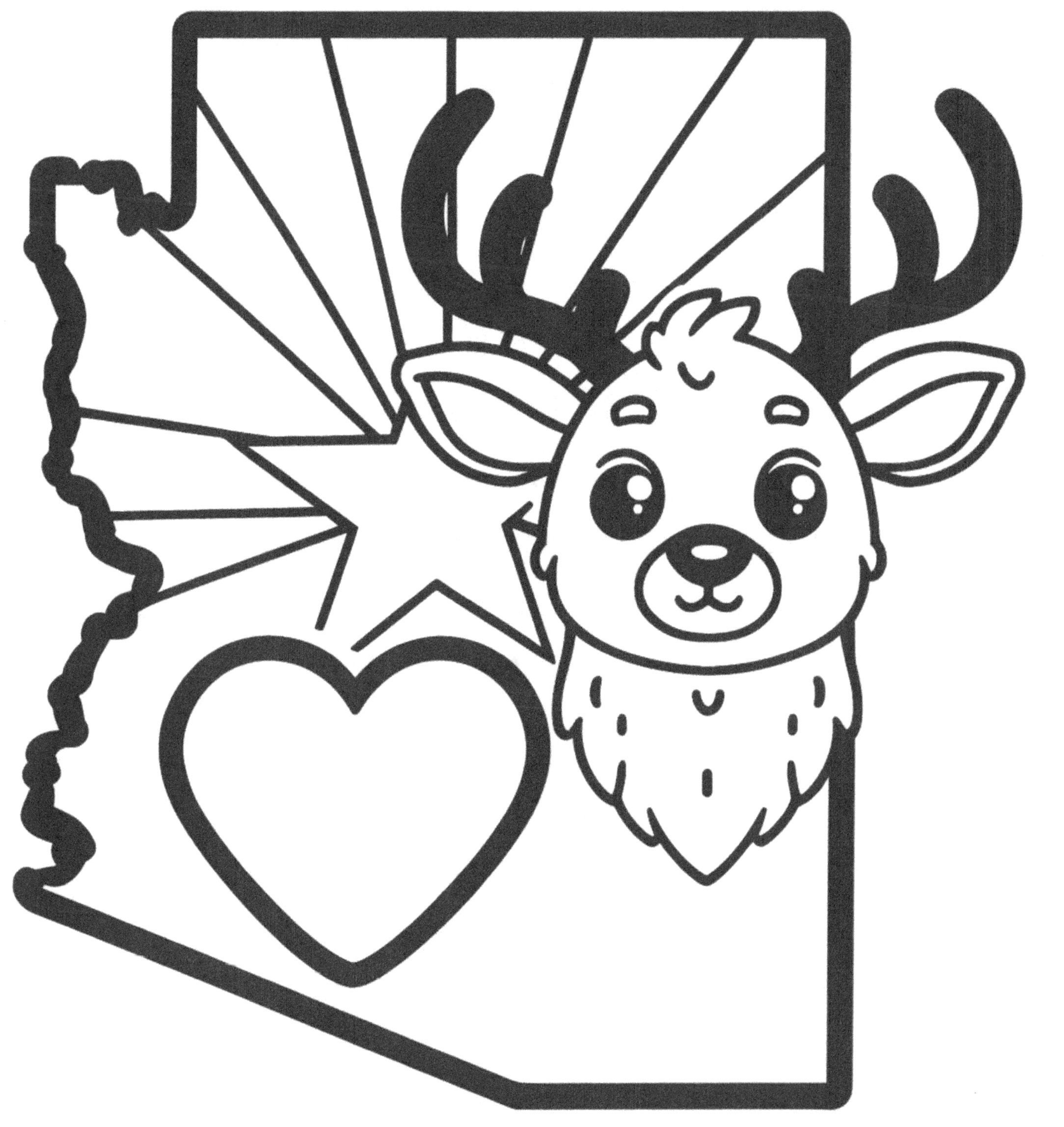

The Ponderosa pine forest in Payson is a magical place filled with tall, majestic trees that smell like vanilla when the sun warms their bark. These trees provide a wonderful home for many animals, including playful squirrels. Squirrels love to scamper up and down the trees, gathering pine cones and storing food for the winter. They are fun to watch as they leap from branch to branch and chatter with their friends.

Question:

Have you ever seen a squirrel in a forest? What do you think the squirrel is doing when it runs up a tree?

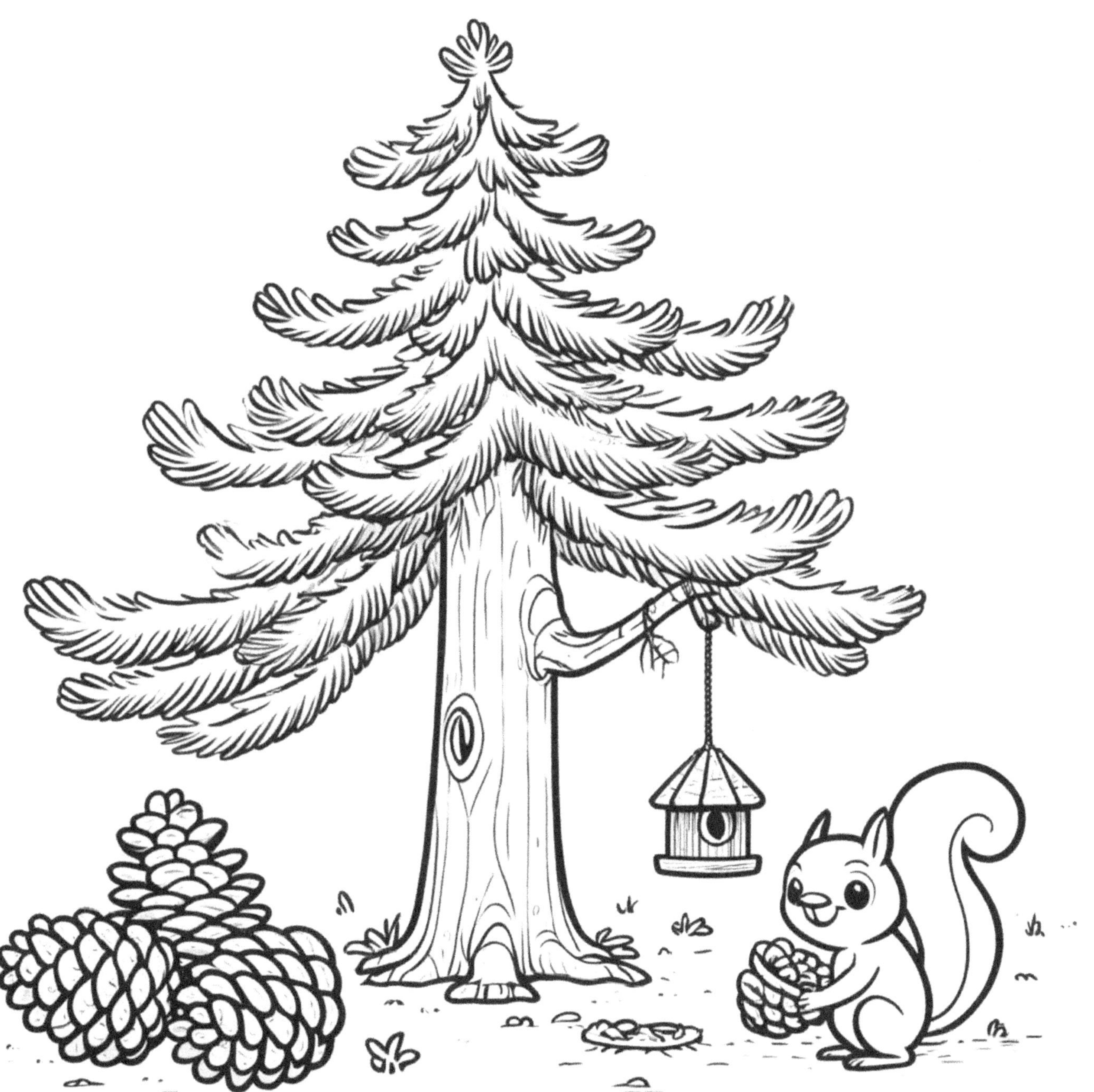

Sunflowers are tall, bright yellow flowers that turn their faces to follow the sun. Bees love sunflowers because they can collect nectar to make honey. You might see a busy bee buzzing around, gathering nectar from the sunflower's center.

Question:

Have you ever seen a bee on a flower? What do you think the bee is doing?

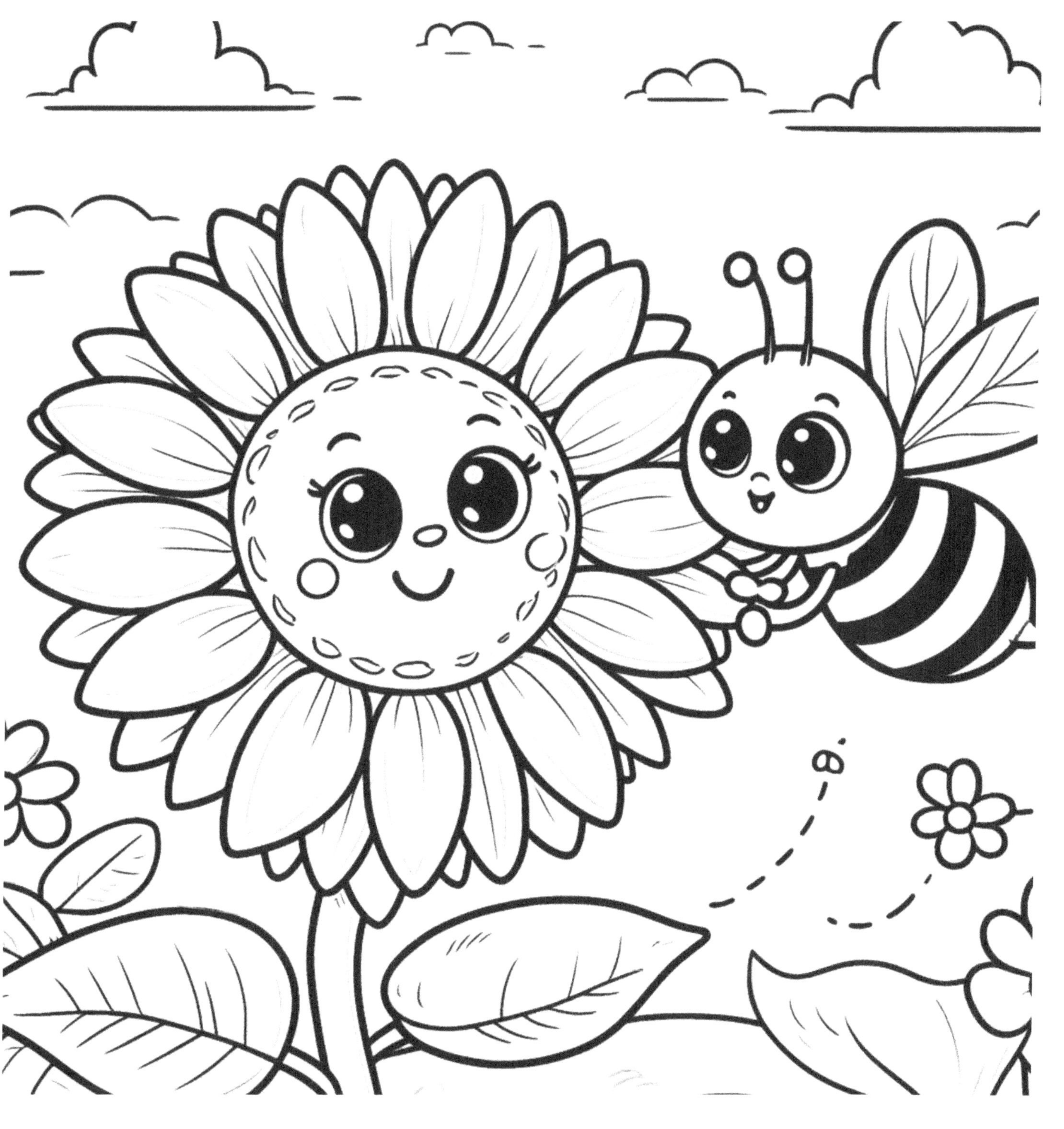

Payson has beautiful golf courses where people can play golf surrounded by nature. The courses are green and lush, and you might even see wildlife while you play. It's a fun way to enjoy the outdoors!

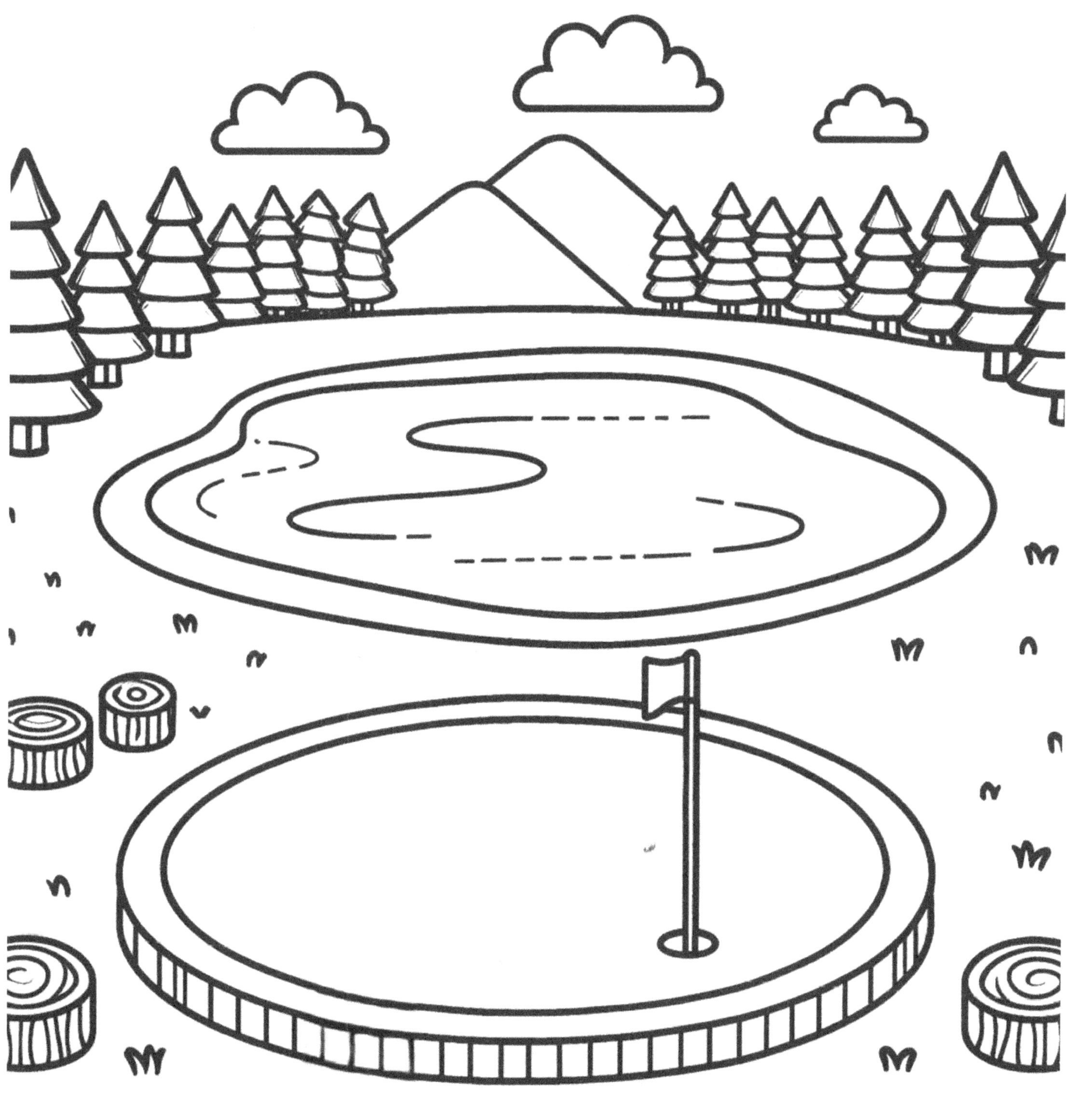

Payson has fun parades with floats, music, and lots of people. You can see colorful costumes, marching bands, and even cowboys and cowgirls riding horses. It's a joyful event that everyone enjoys.

Question:

Have you ever been to a parade?

What was your favorite part?

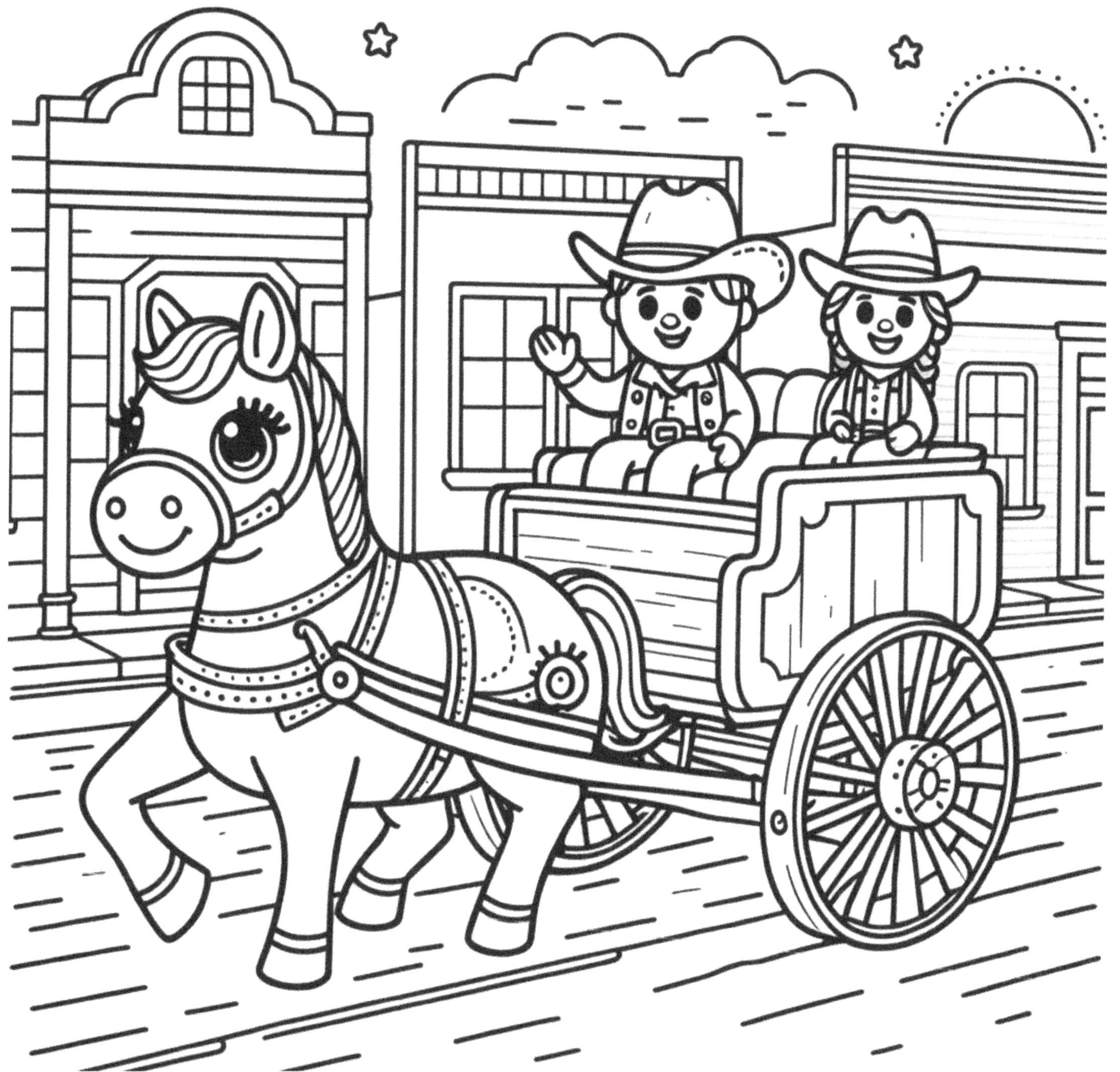

Rodeo clowns in Payson are funny and brave. They dress in colorful clothes and make people laugh, but they also help keep bull riders safe during the rodeo. It's an exciting and important job!

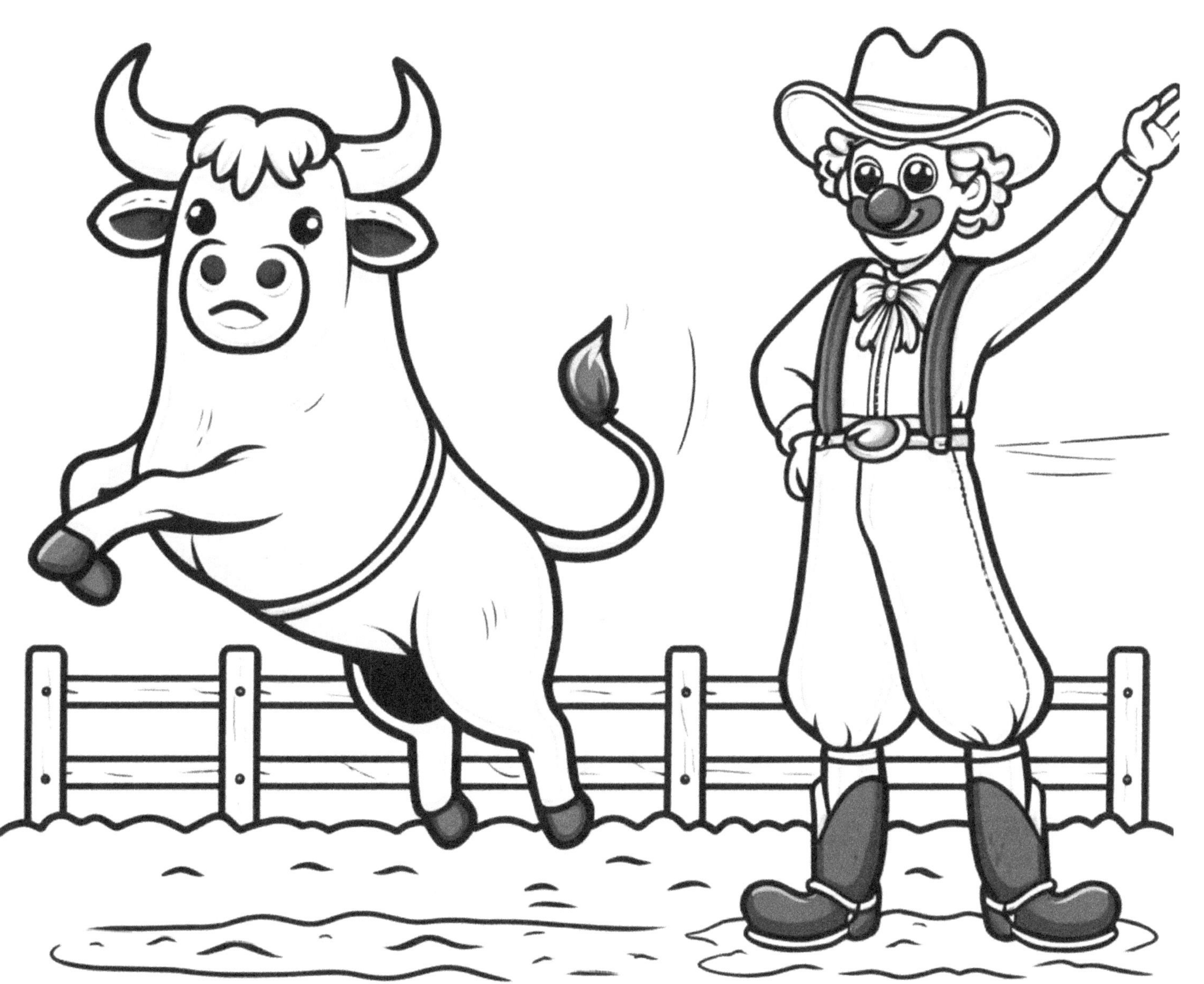

In Payson, you can see amazing cowgirls at the rodeo. Cowgirls are skilled riders who perform incredible tricks on horseback. They can race around barrels, rope cattle, and ride with great speed and control. They wear colorful outfits and hats, making their performances even more exciting to watch.

Question:

Would you like to learn how to
ride a horse like a cowgirl?
What kind of trick would you want to try?

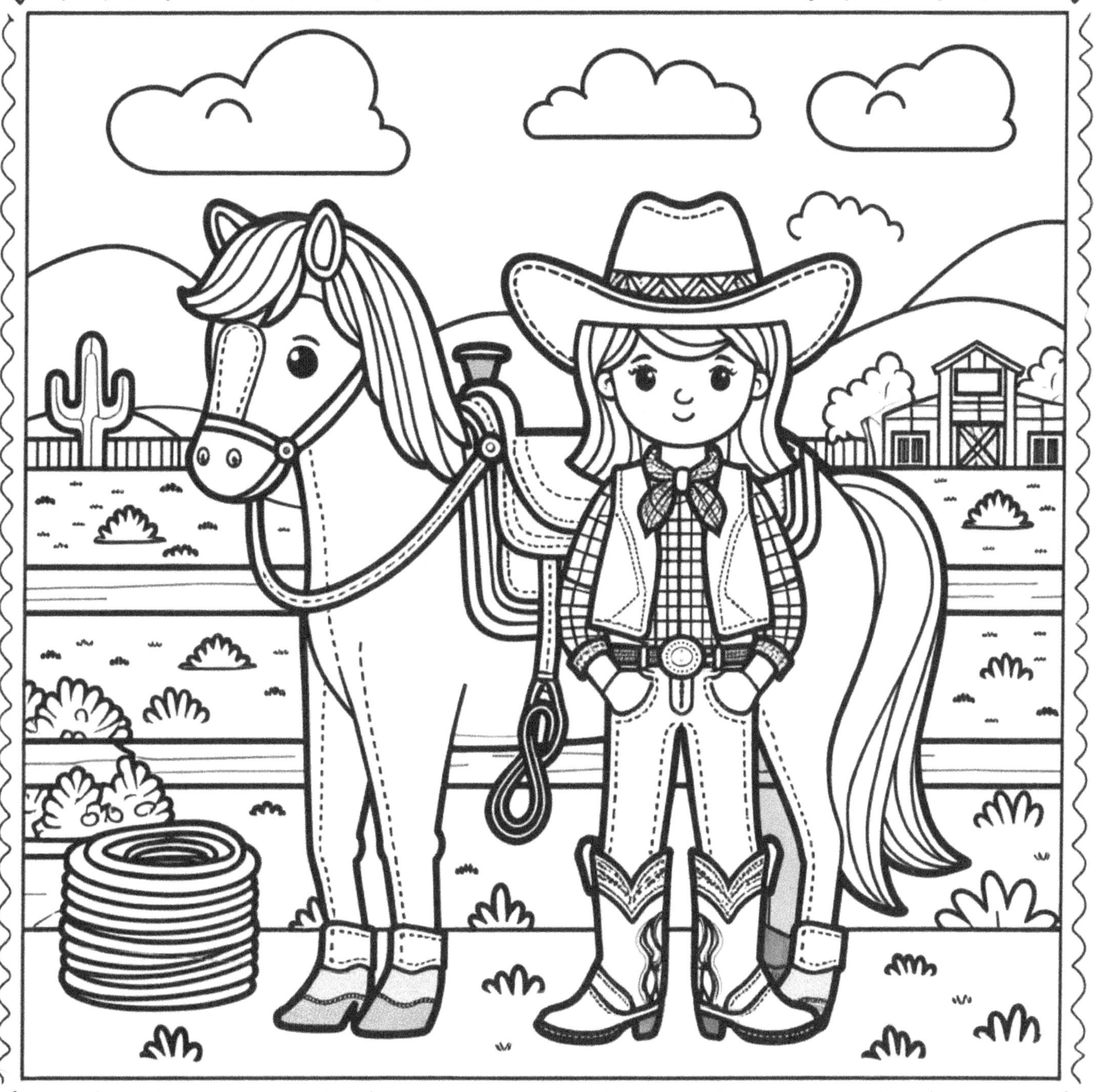

Bull riding is one of the most thrilling events at the rodeo in Payson. Bull riders are brave individuals who try to stay on a bucking bull for as long as they can. They wear protective gear and hold onto the bull with one hand while the bull jumps and twists. It's an exciting challenge that takes a lot of courage and skill.

Question:

Do you think you would be brave enough to ride a bucking bull?

How long do you think you could stay on?

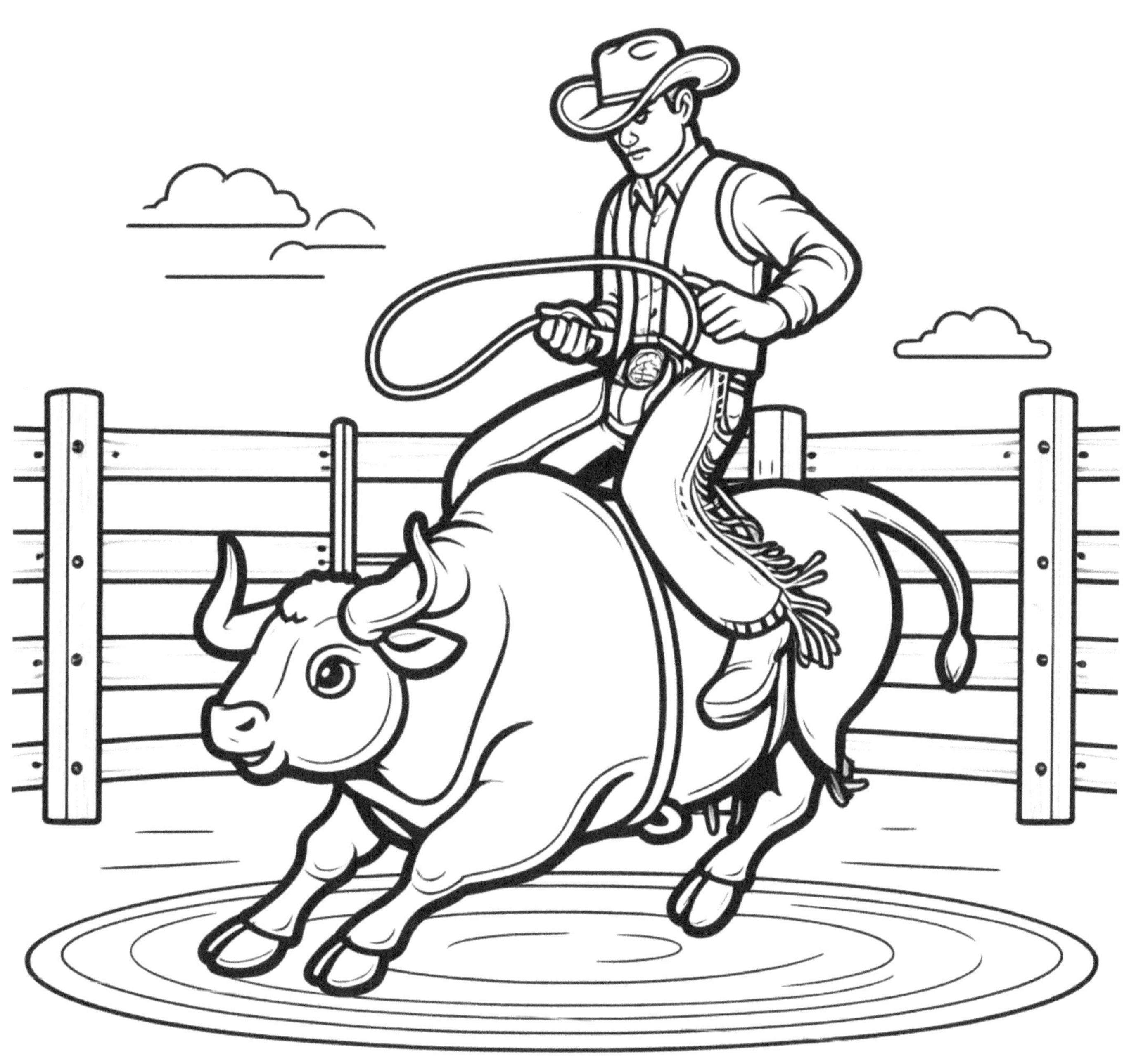

Off-roading is an exciting adventure where you drive a special vehicle over rough terrain like dirt trails and rocky paths. In Payson, you can go off-roading with your dad and explore the great outdoors, bouncing over bumps and splashing through puddles.

Question:
Would you like to go off-roading?
What kind of things do you think you would see on the trail?

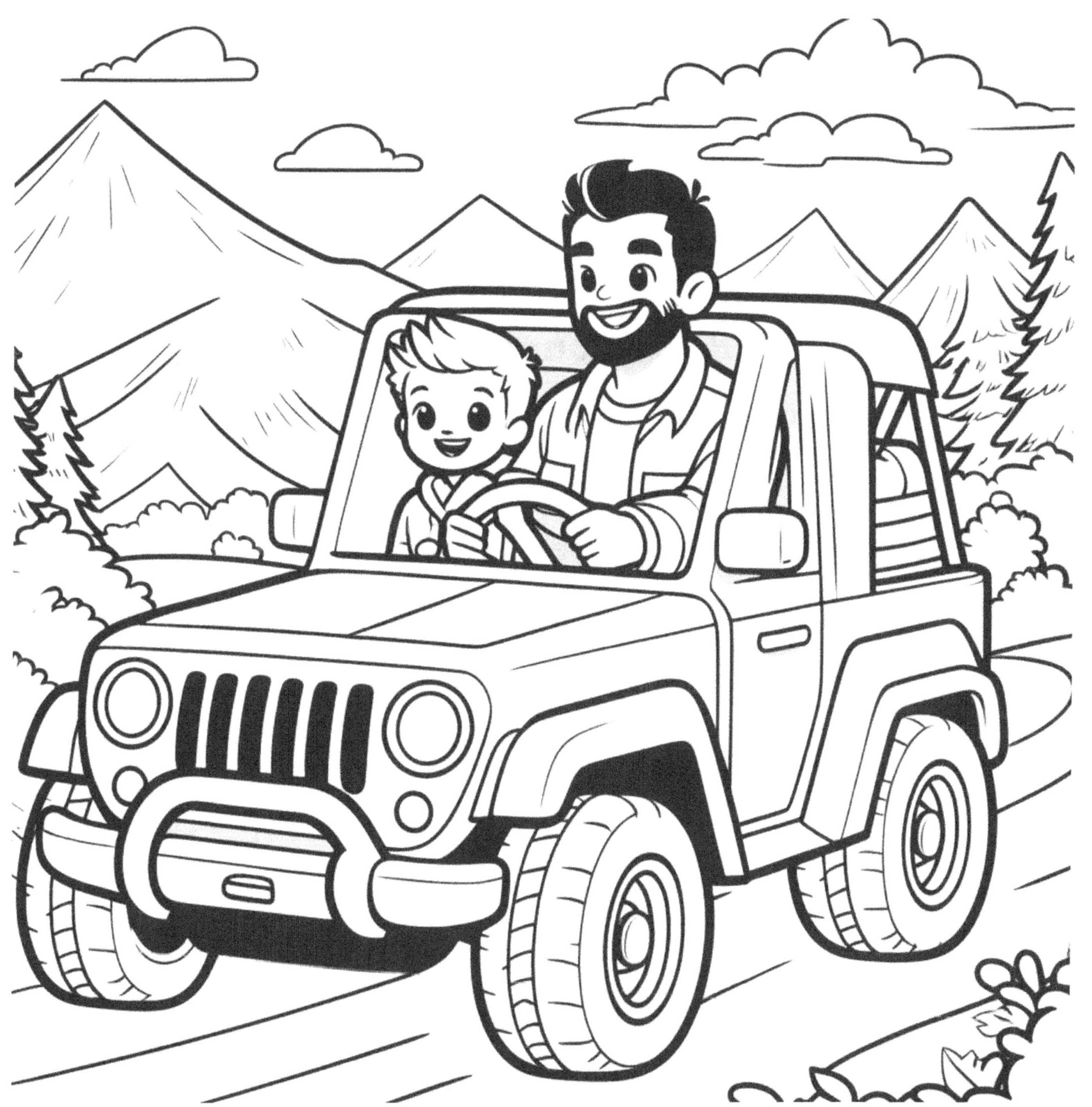

The Pony Express was a famous mail delivery service that started in 1860. Brave riders on fast horses carried mail across the country, traveling day and night through all kinds of weather. In Payson, you can learn about the Pony Express and how it played a part in history. Riders would gallop through the rugged landscapes, delivering important messages and letters. It was a daring and adventurous job that helped connect people across long distances.

Question:

Can you imagine riding a horse to deliver mail? What kind of messages would you like to carry on your journey?

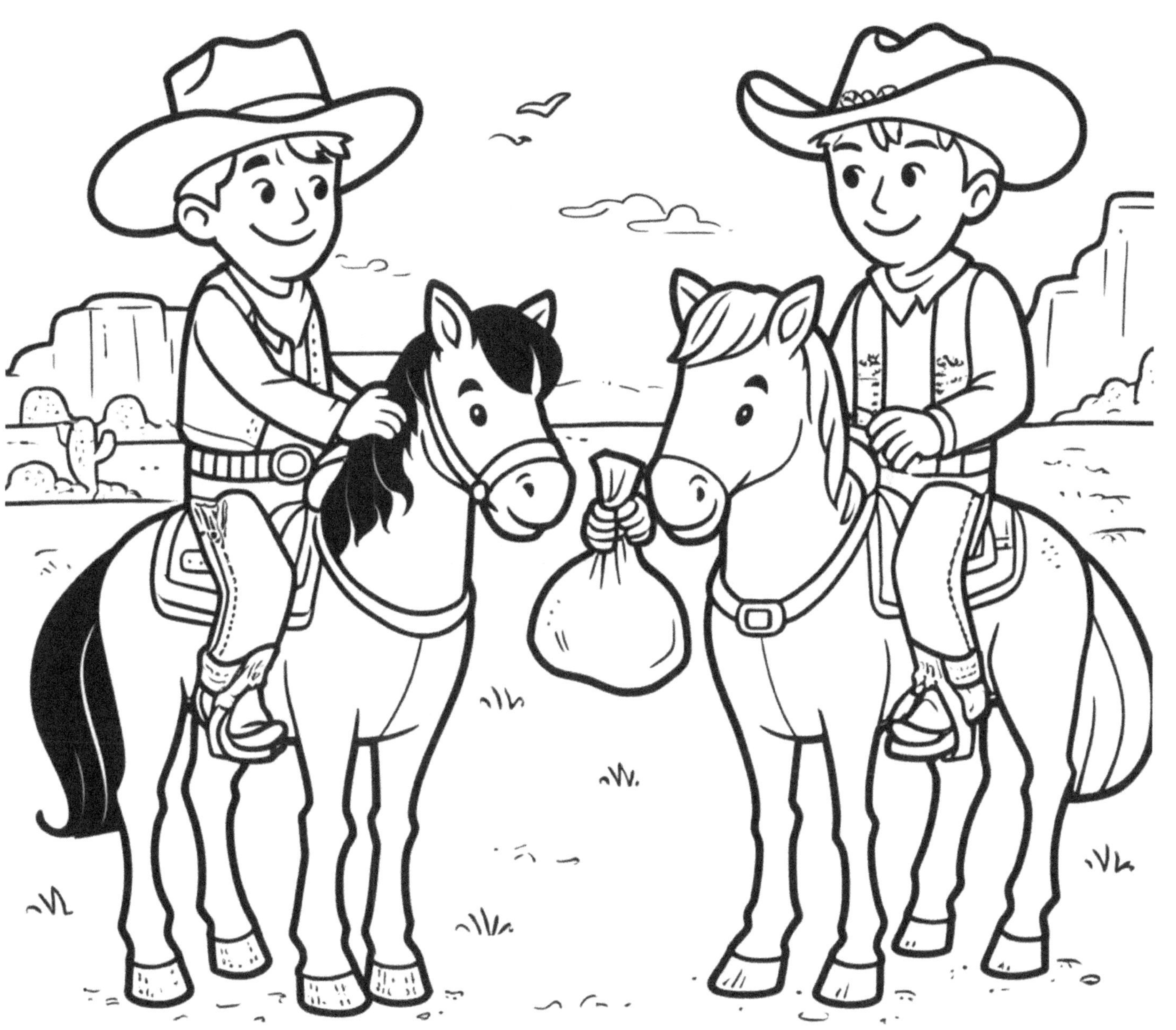

At the honey stand in Rim Country, you can taste different kinds of honey made by local bees. There's wildflower honey, clover honey, and more. Honey is sweet and delicious, and it's fun to try different flavors.

Question:

Do you like honey?

What do you like to eat honey with?

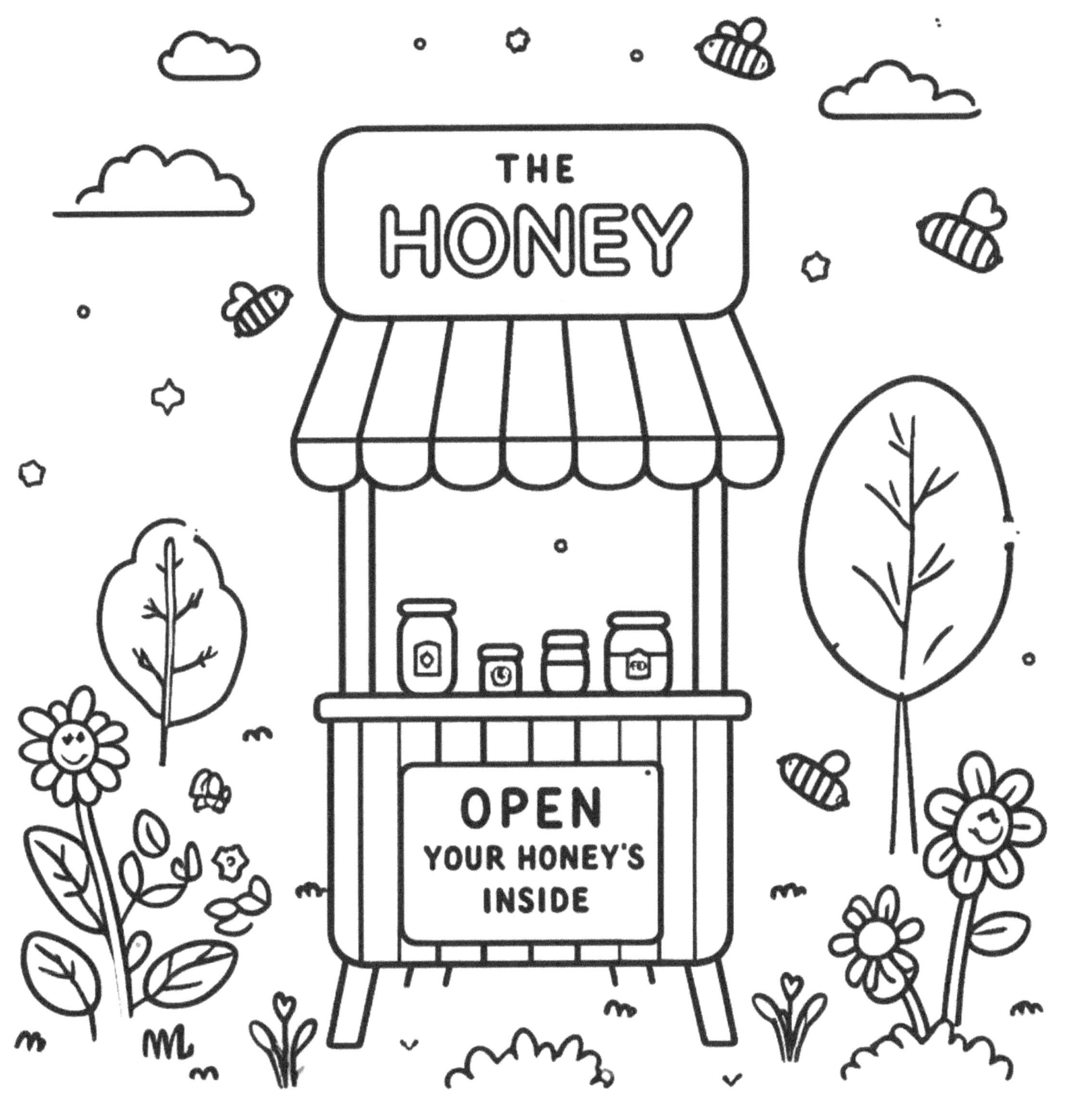

THE
HONEY
OPEN
YOUR HONEY'S
INSIDE

Payson has many great swimming pools where kids can cool off and have fun.
Whether it's at a local park, a community center, or even a backyard pool, swimming is a great way to enjoy a sunny day.
You can splash, dive, and float in the water, play with friends, and even practice swimming like a fish.
Some pools have slides and fountains that make swimming even more exciting!

Question:

What is your favorite thing to do at the swimming pool? Do you like to splash, dive, or just float around?

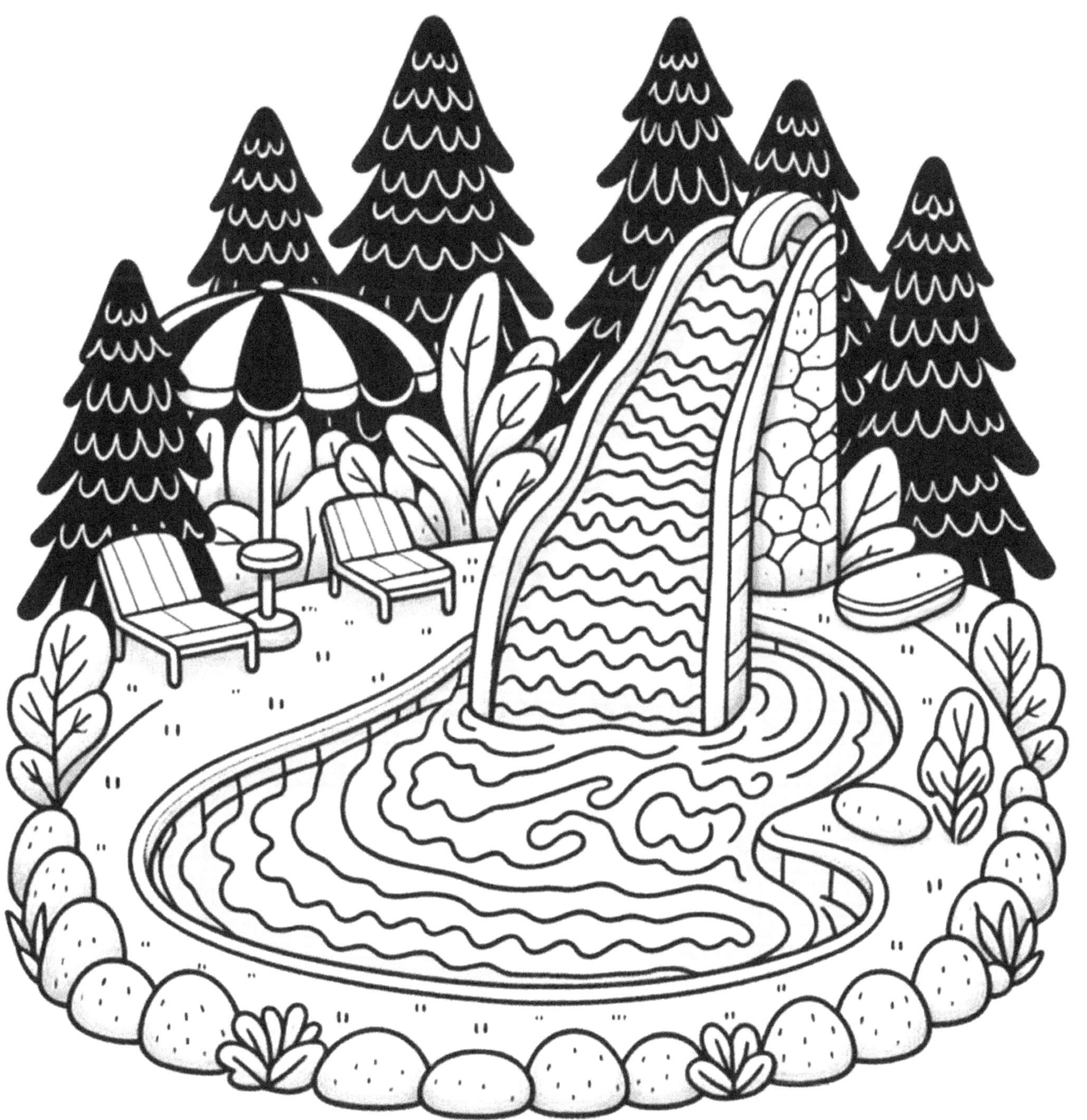

Hiking in Payson is a wonderful adventure. There are many trails that wind through forests and along streams. You can explore and discover all sorts of plants and animals. Don't forget to bring your dog along for some company!

Question:

Do you like going on walks with your dog? Where is your favorite place to explore?

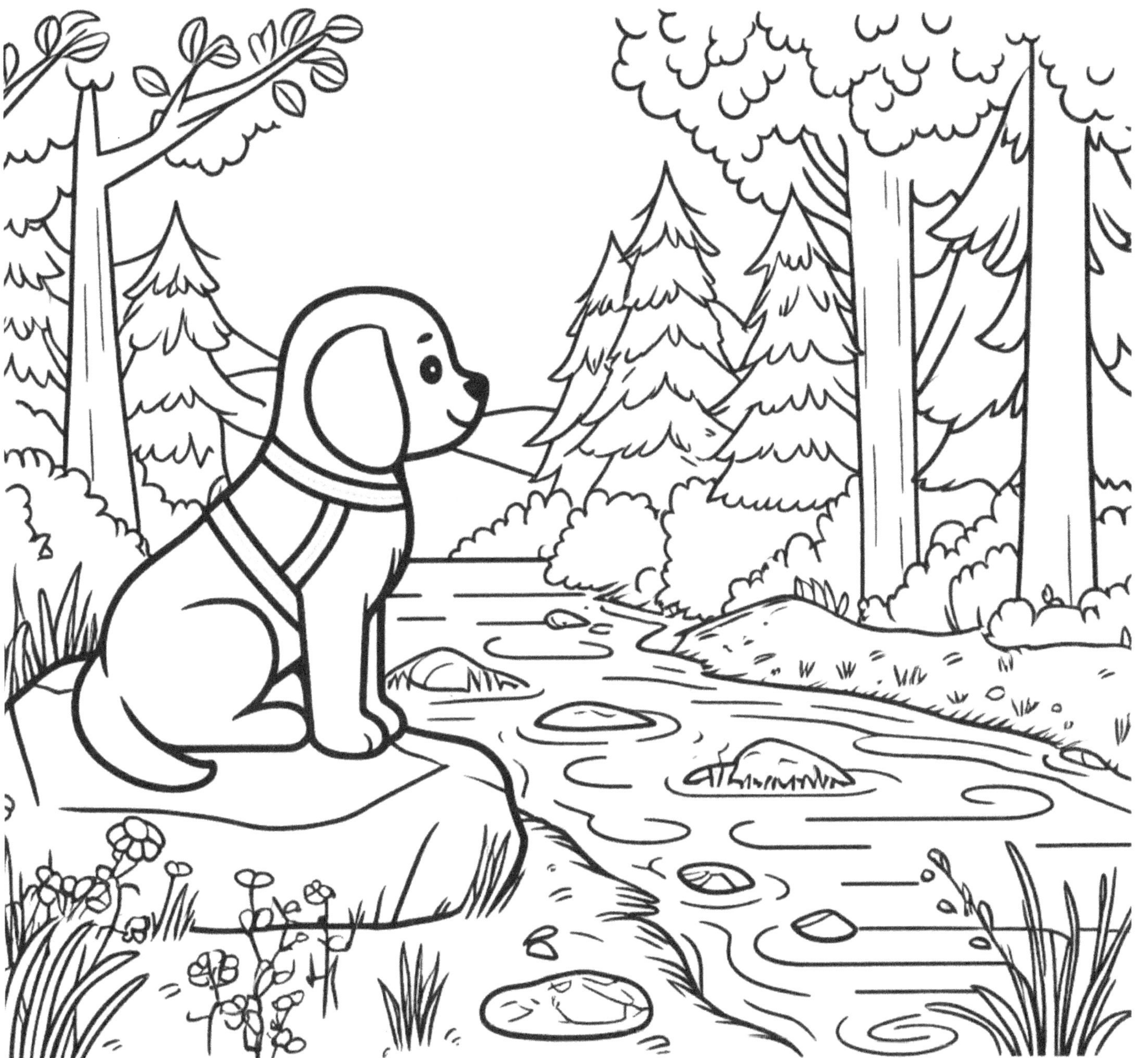

The Water Wheel hike off Houston Mesa Road in Payson is a beautiful adventure. This trail takes you along the East Verde River, where you can see sparkling water, rocky cascades, and lush greenery. The highlight of the hike is the old water wheel, a remnant of Payson's history. Kids love to splash in the river's pools and explore the natural beauty all around.

Question:

Would you like to hike along a river and find an old water wheel? What do you think you'd see along the way?

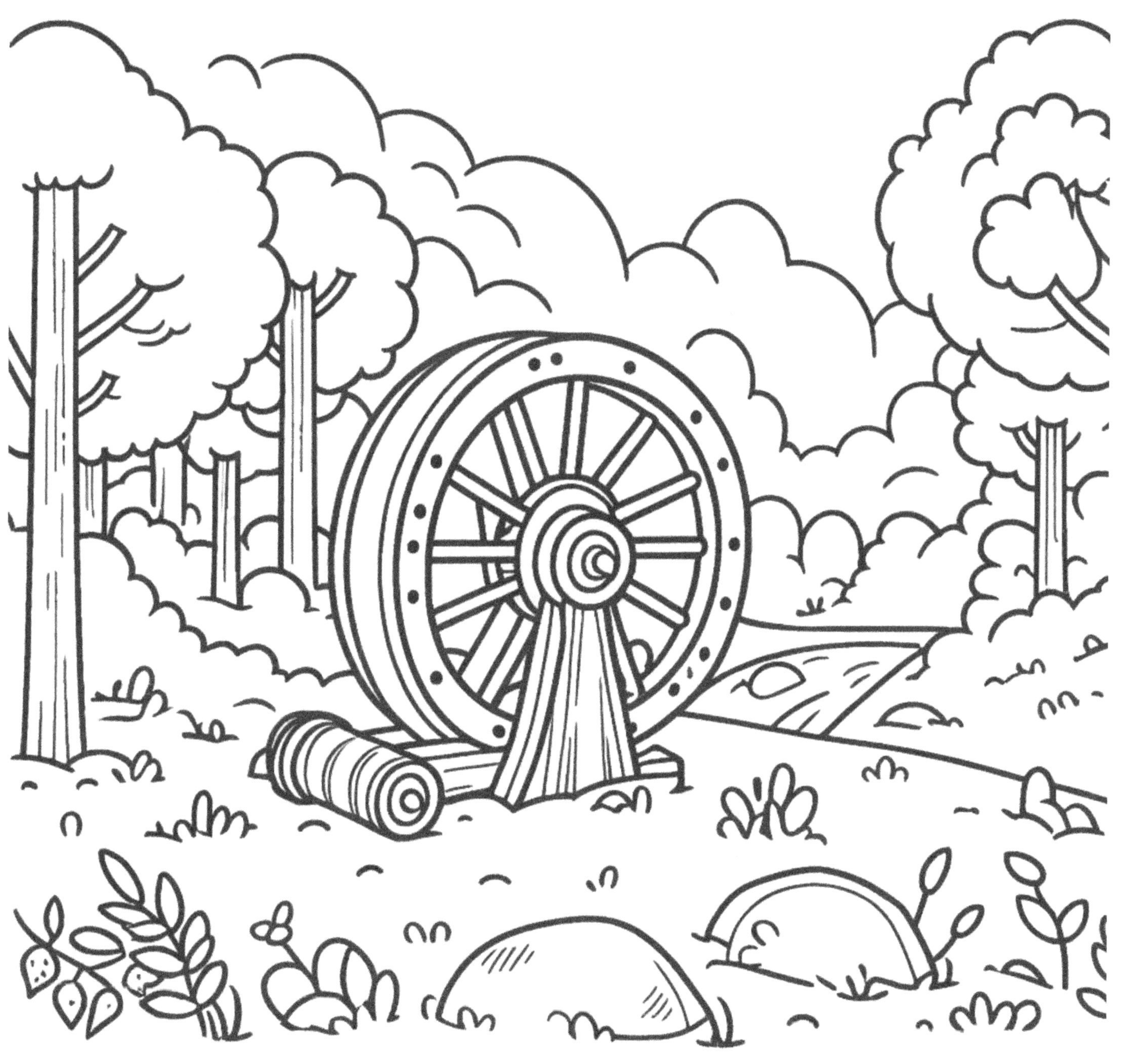

The Natural Bridge, located near Payson, is a stunning natural wonder. It's one of the largest natural travertine bridges in the world. The bridge is made of rock and spans Pine Creek, creating a beautiful archway that you can hike under. Visitors love to explore the area, take pictures, and marvel at the impressive formation.

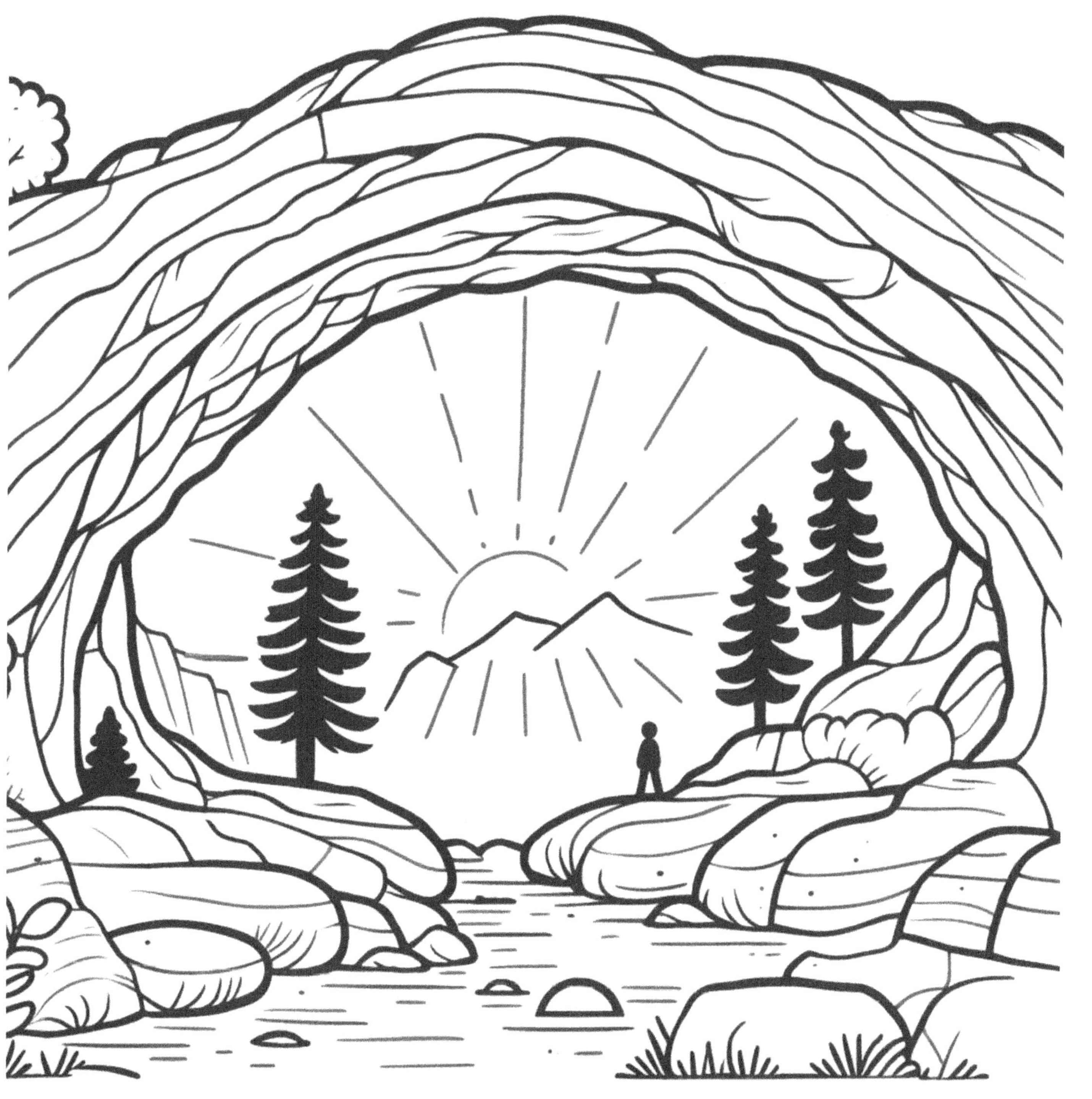

Off Baby Doll Road in Payson, you might spot a majestic steer grazing in the fields. Steers are large, strong cattle that are often seen on ranches. They have big, curved horns and a calm demeanor. Watching a steer up close can be a fascinating experience, seeing how they move and graze.

Question:
Have you ever seen a steer up close? What would you do if you saw one while exploring?

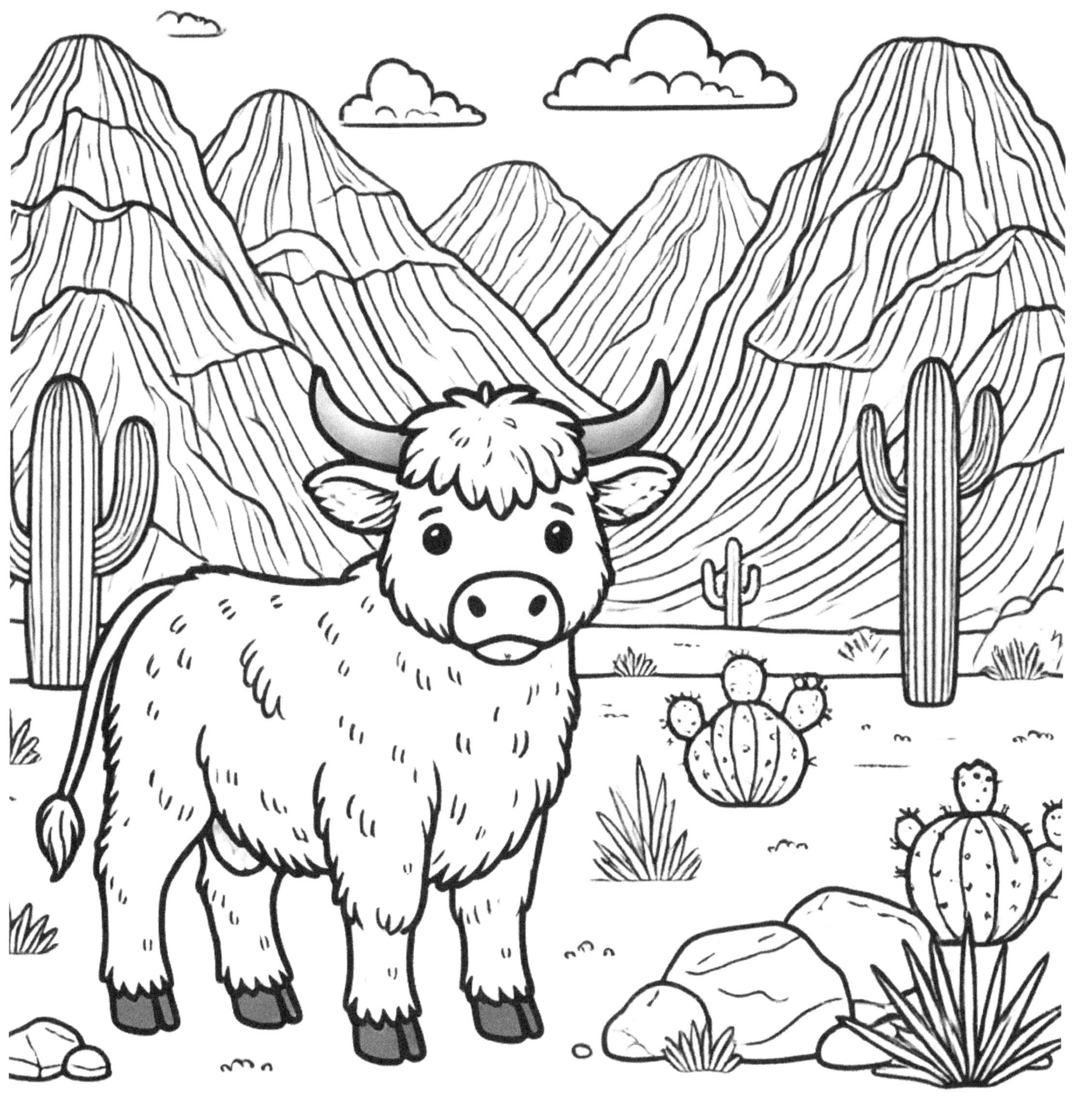

Payson has parks with lakes where you can go fishing. It's a peaceful way to spend the day. You can sit by the water, cast your fishing line, and maybe catch a fish or two!

Question:

Have you ever been fishing?

What would you do if you caught a fish?

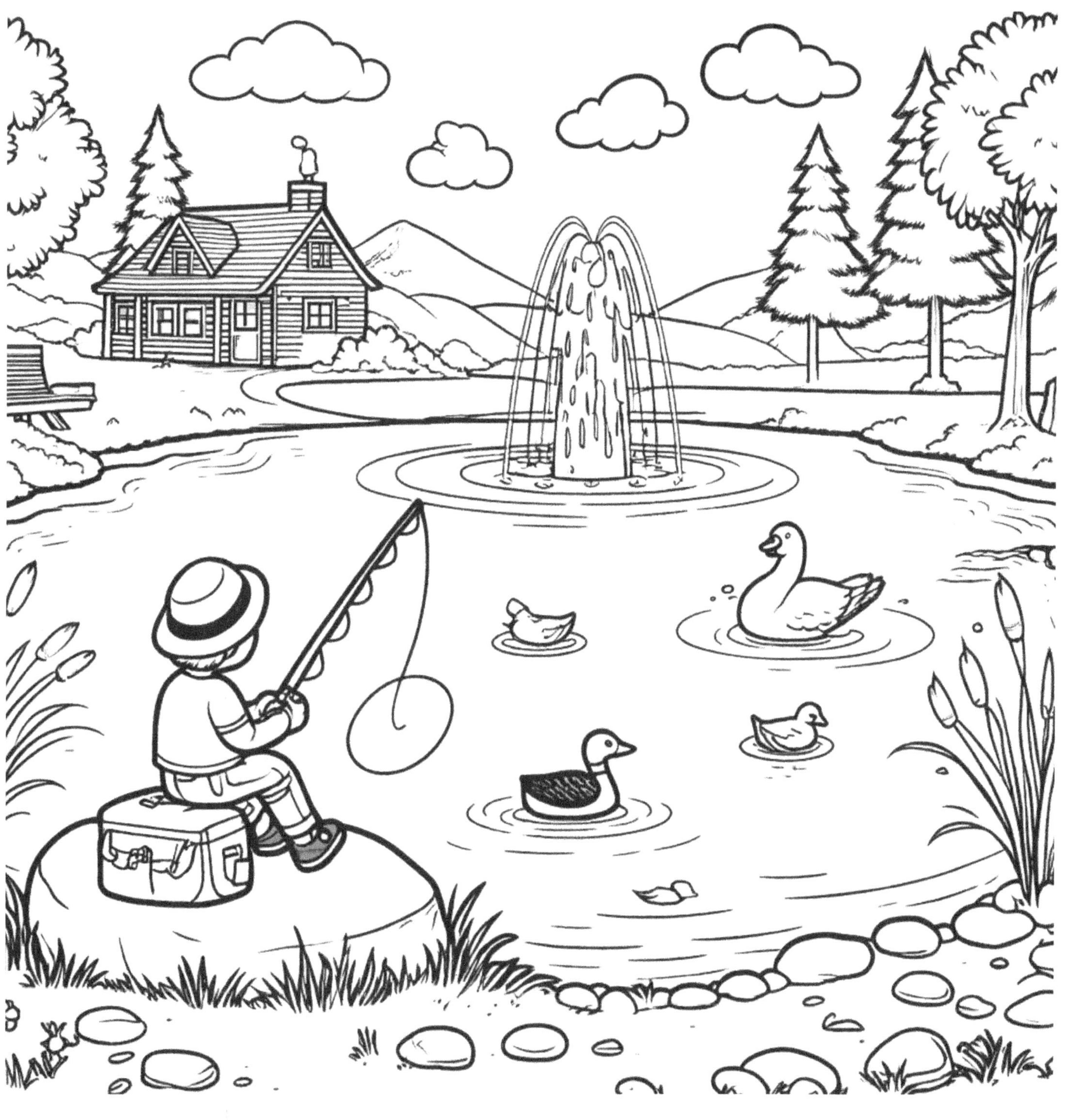

Payson's neighbor Pine, has a beautiful lavender farm where you can see rows of purple flowers. Lavender smells wonderful and is used in soaps, lotions, and even in food. Visiting a lavender farm is a calming experience.

Question:

Have you ever smelled lavender?

What's your favorite flower?

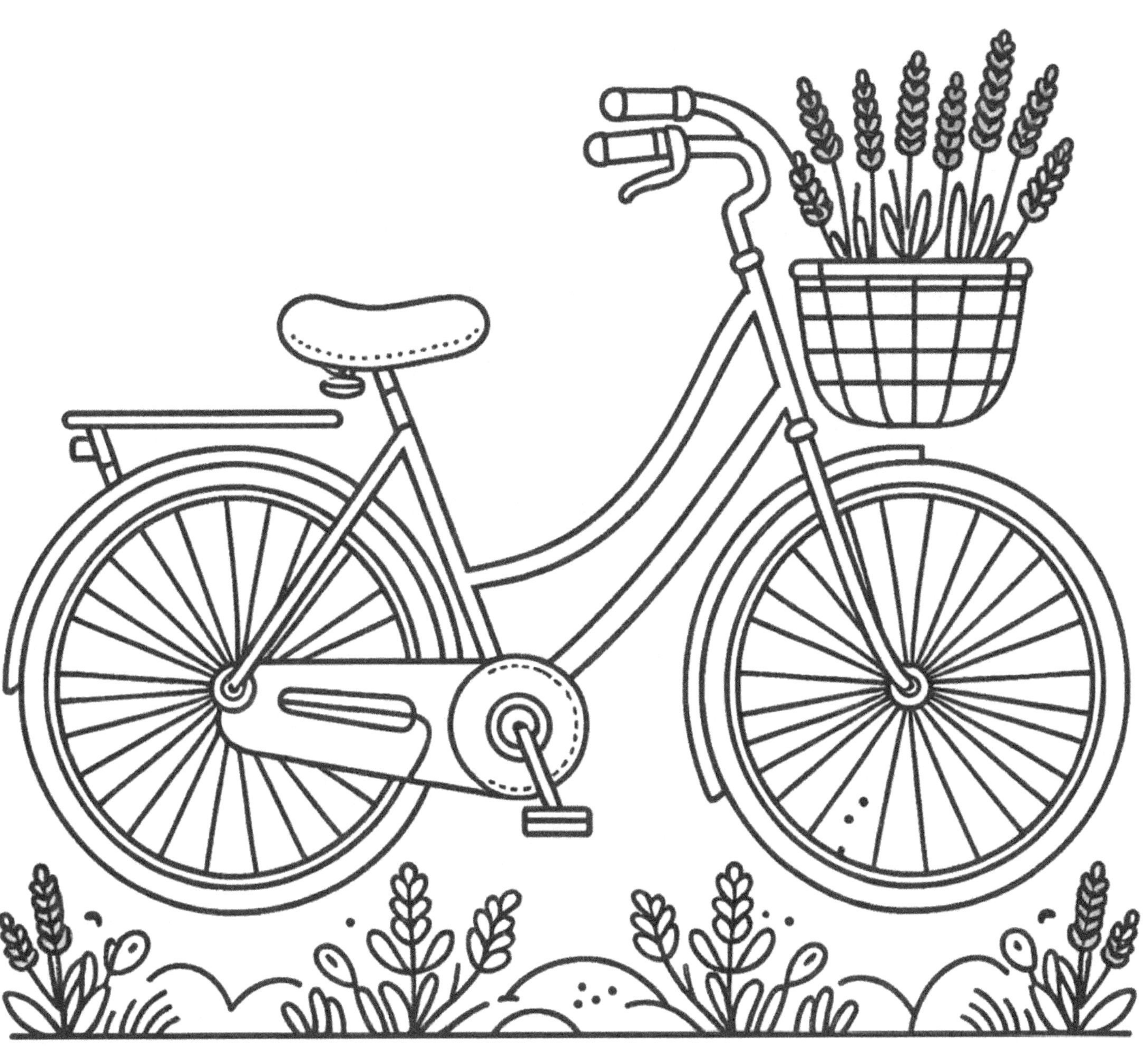

Riding horses is a fun activity in Payson. Kids can learn to ride horses at ranches and farms, enjoying the fresh air and beautiful scenery. Horses are gentle and friendly, and riding them can make you feel like a real cowboy or cowgirl.

Question:

Have you ever ridden a horse? What would you name your horse if you had one?

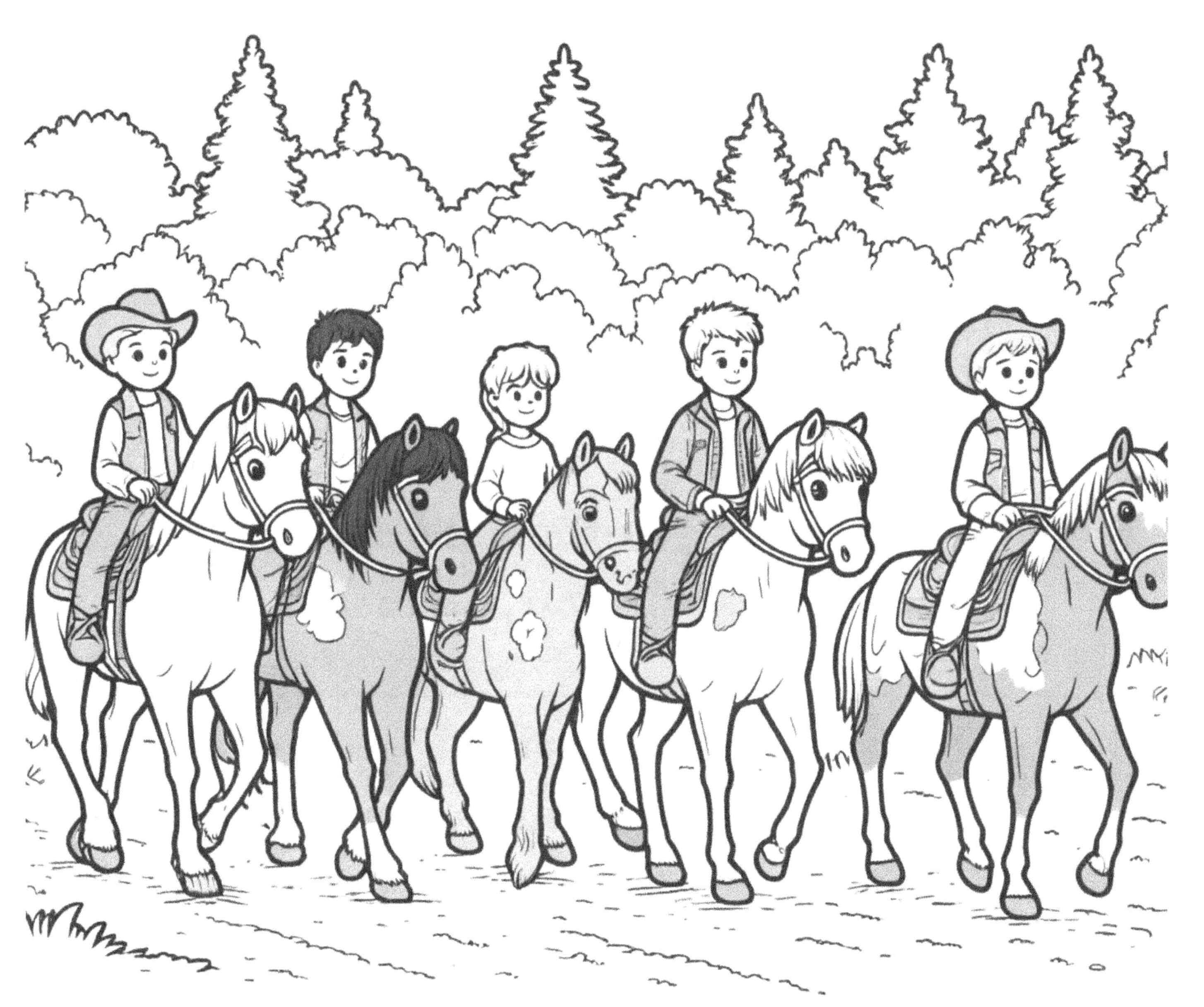

Elk are large, graceful animals that live in the forests around Payson. They have big antlers and make a bugling sound in the fall. Sometimes, you can see them grazing in the meadows early in the morning or late in the evening.
Make sure you give them the space they need to keep both you and them safe!

Question:
Can you imagine seeing a big elk with huge antlers while you're out for a walk?

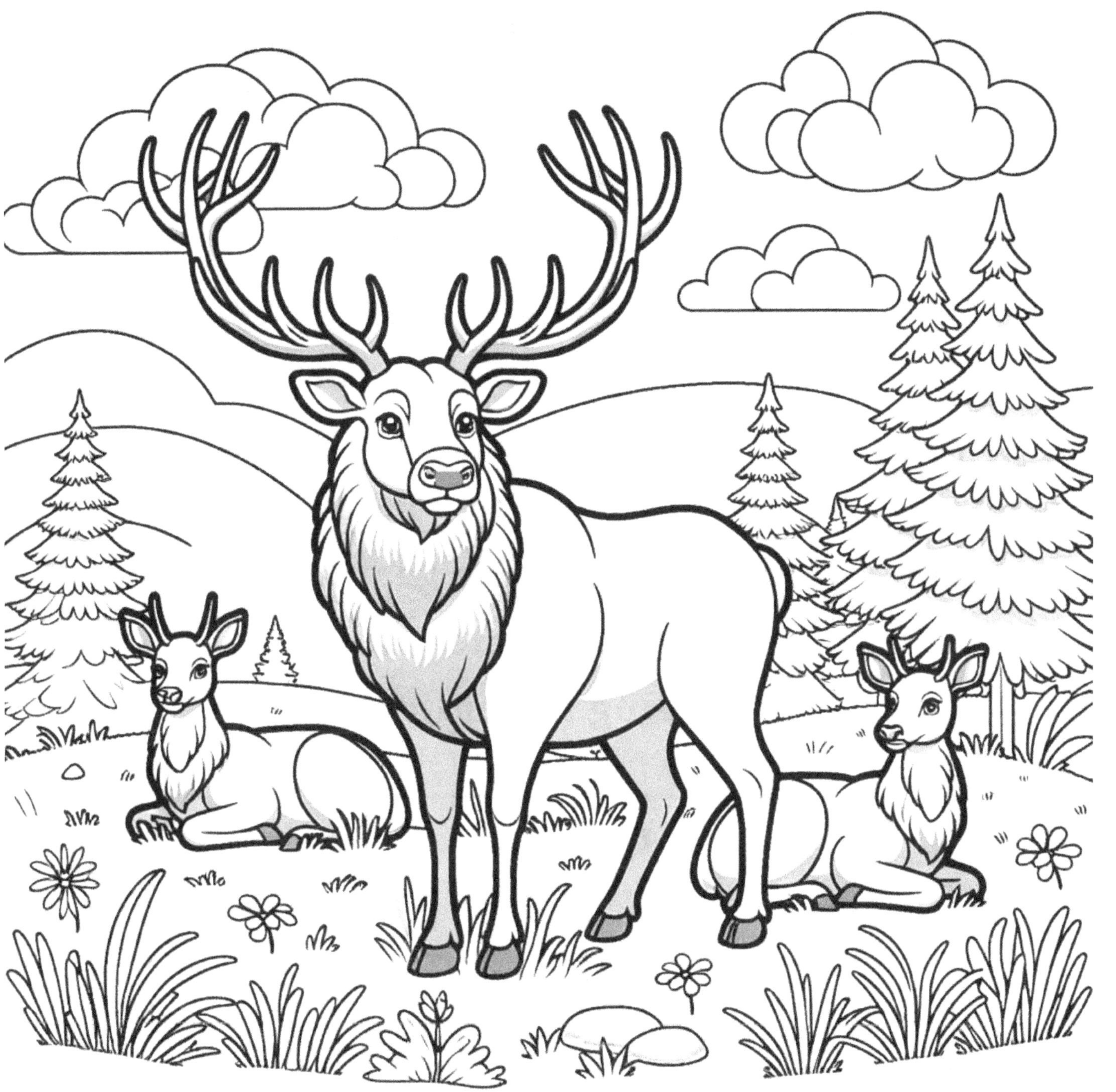

Camping in Payson is a fantastic adventure! You can set up a tent in the beautiful forests or by a clear, flowing stream. Camping is even more fun when you bring your pet along. Pets love exploring new places and enjoying nature with you. It's important to remember to clean up your campsite before you leave. Picking up trash and packing away all your gear helps keep the forest clean and safe for everyone, including the animals.

Question:

Have you ever gone camping with your pet? What do you think your pet would like best about camping?

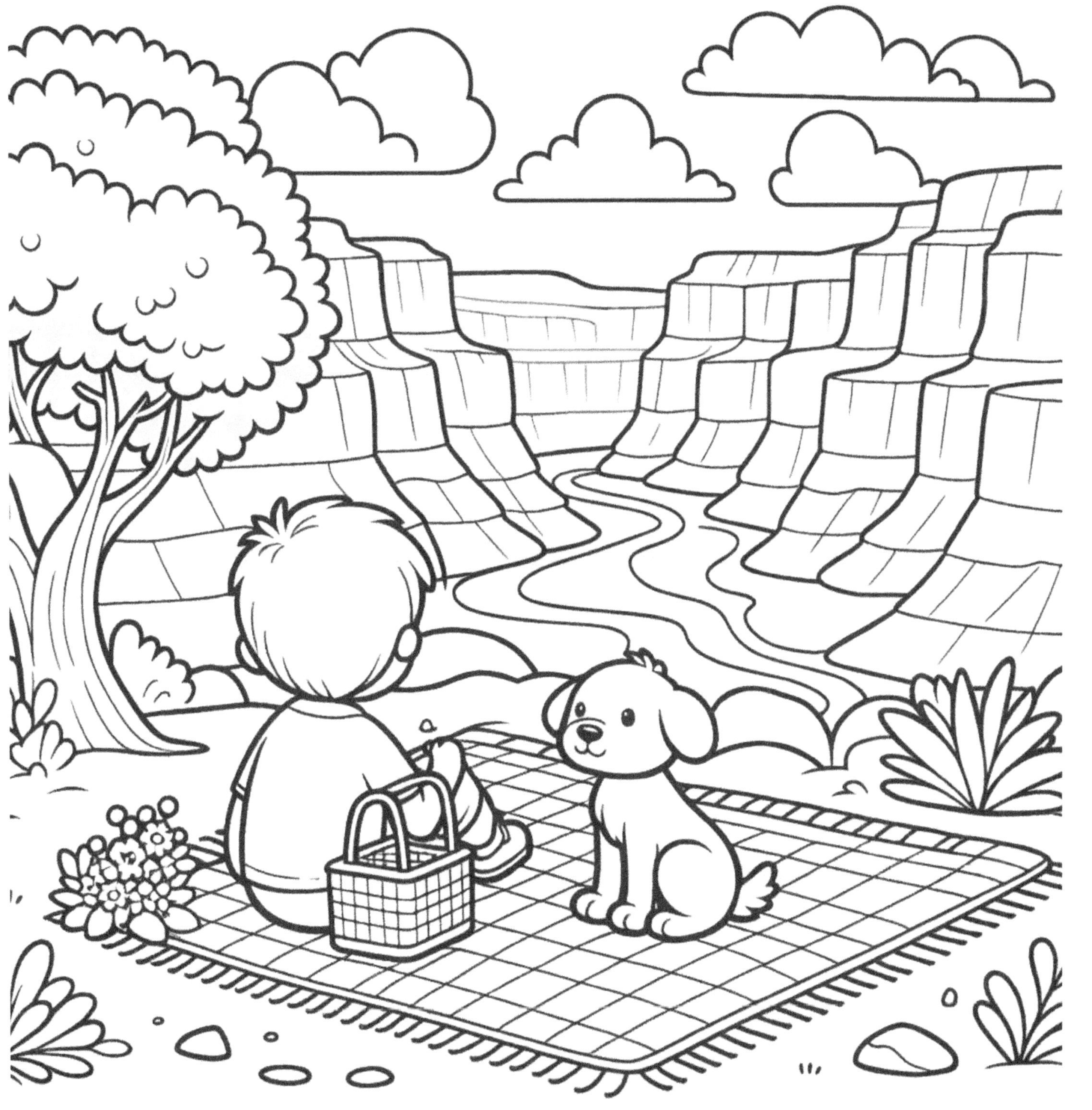

The whiskered screech owl is a tiny, mysterious bird with large eyes and whisker-like feathers around its face. These owls live in the forests around Payson and are usually seen at night. They make a soft, trilling sound that echoes through the trees. If you listen carefully during a quiet evening, you might hear one calling out.

Question:

Have you ever heard an owl at night?

What do you think it sounds like?

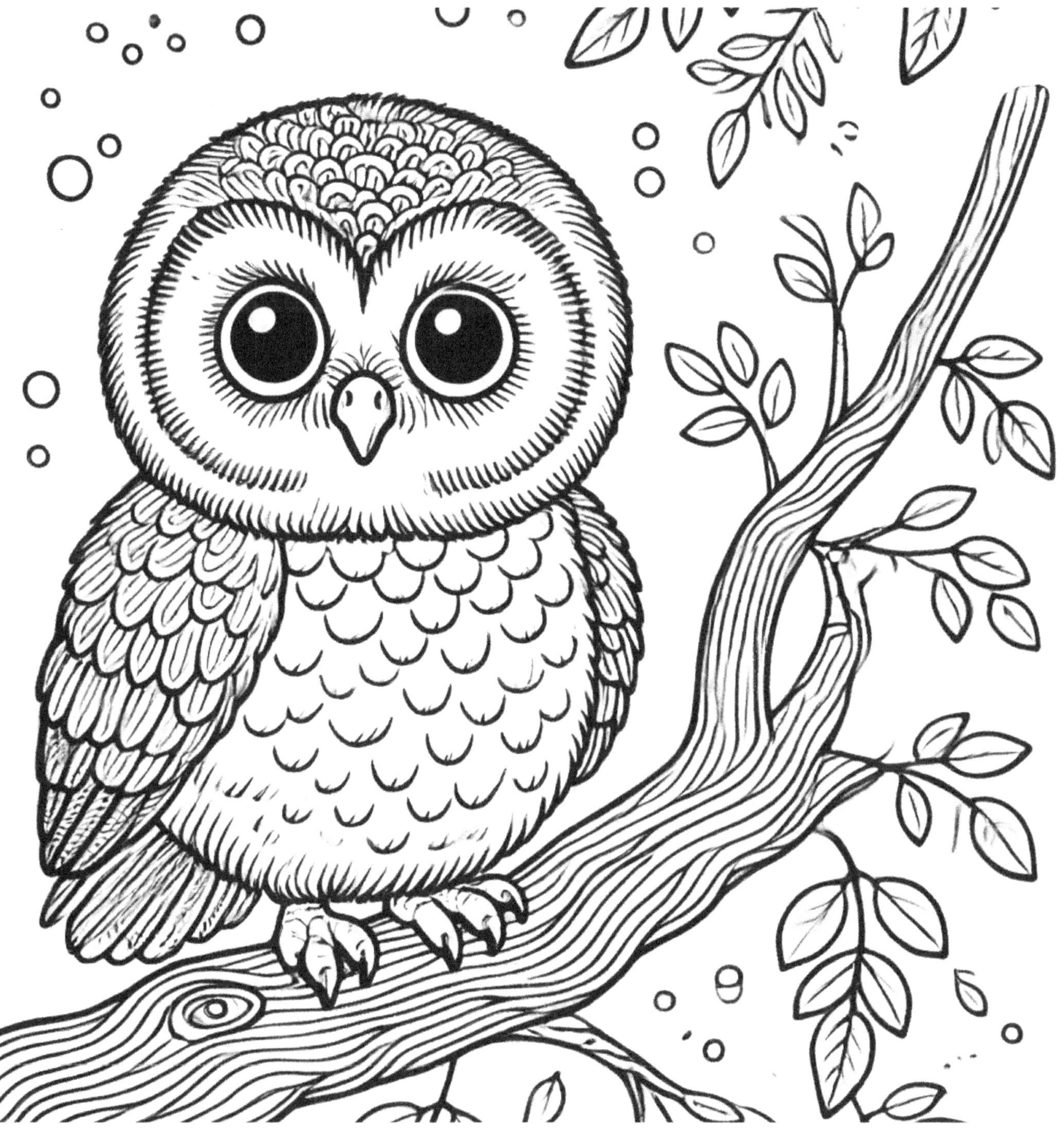

Javelinas are interesting animals that look a bit like wild pigs but are actually more closely related to hippos! In Payson, you can sometimes see a mother javelina walking with her babies. They have short, bristly fur and small tusks. Javelinas love to eat plants, roots, and fruits.

Question:
Would you like to see a javelina family? What do you think the baby javelinas like to eat the most?

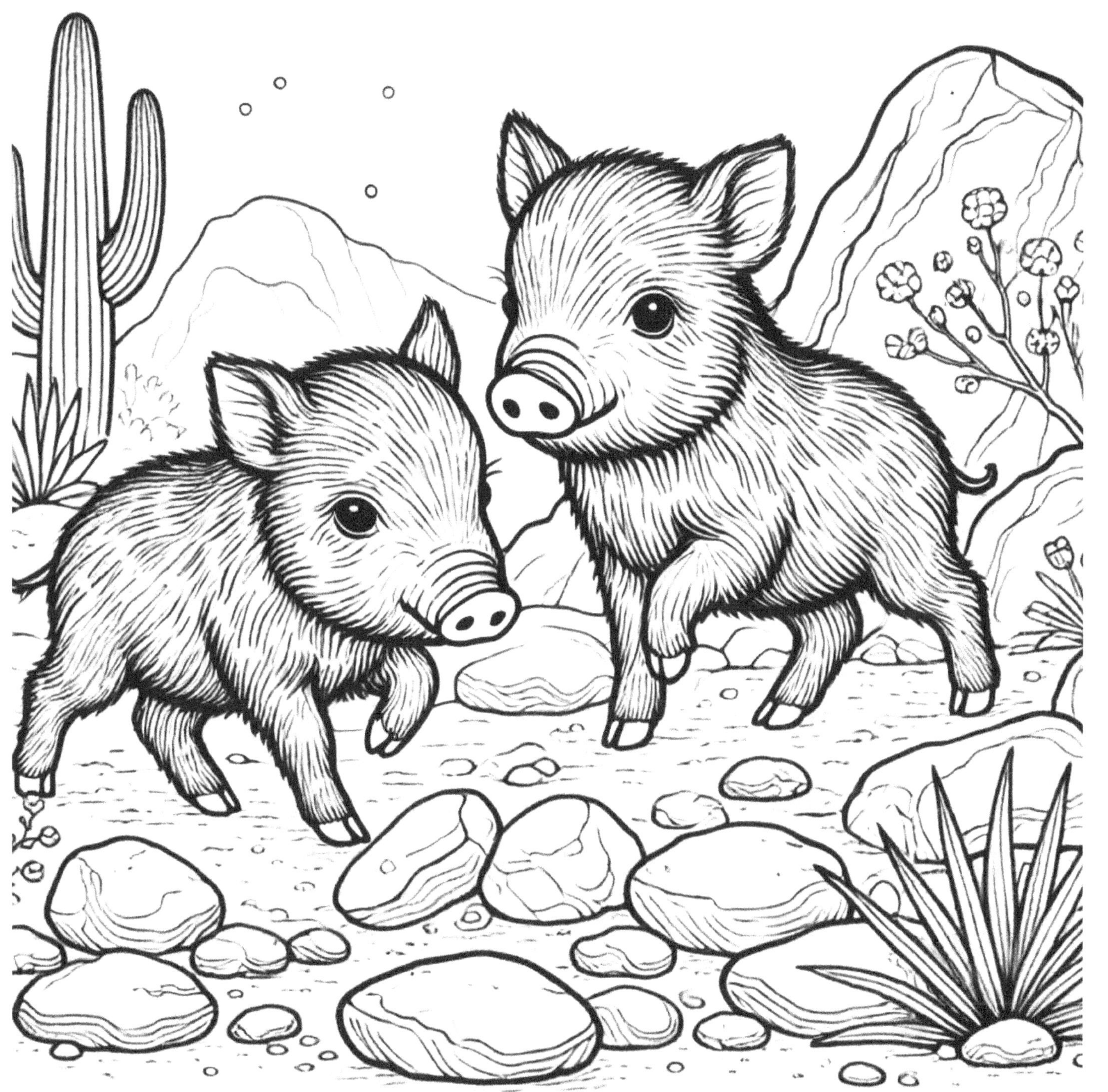

The mountain lion, also known as a cougar or puma, is a powerful and graceful animal that lives in the mountains and forests around Payson. These big cats have tan fur, sharp claws, and long tails. They are excellent hunters and can run, jump, and climb very well. Although they are shy and usually stay away from people, it's exciting to know they are out there in the wild.

Question:

Can you imagine seeing a mountain lion in the wild? What would you do if you spotted one from a safe distance?

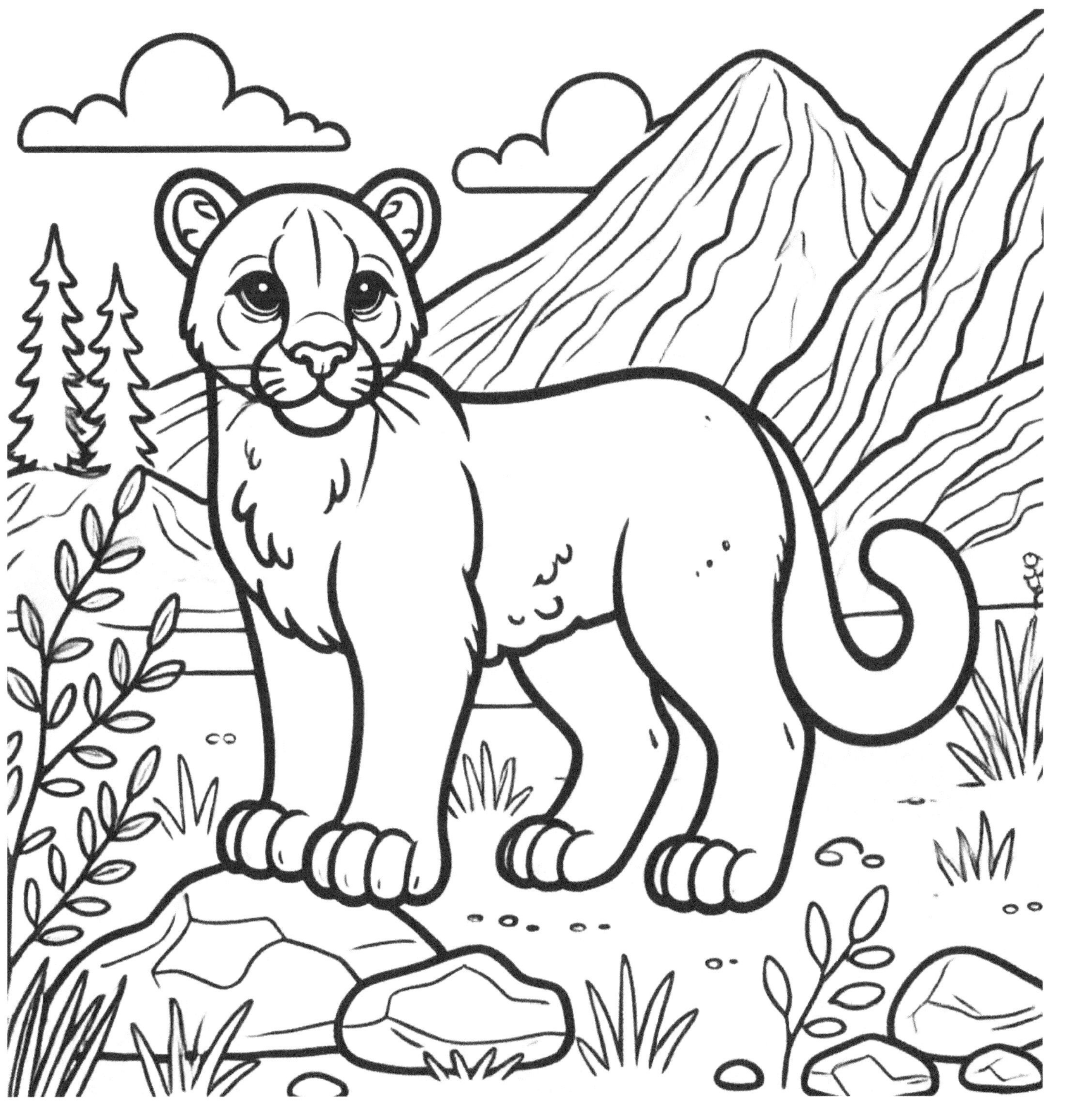

Coyotes are clever and curious animals that live in the wild areas around Payson. At night, you might hear their howls echoing through the hills. Coyotes use their howls to communicate with each other, almost like they're talking. They look like small, wild dogs with pointy ears and bushy tails.

Question:

Can you imagine hearing a coyote howl? What do you think they might be saying to each other?

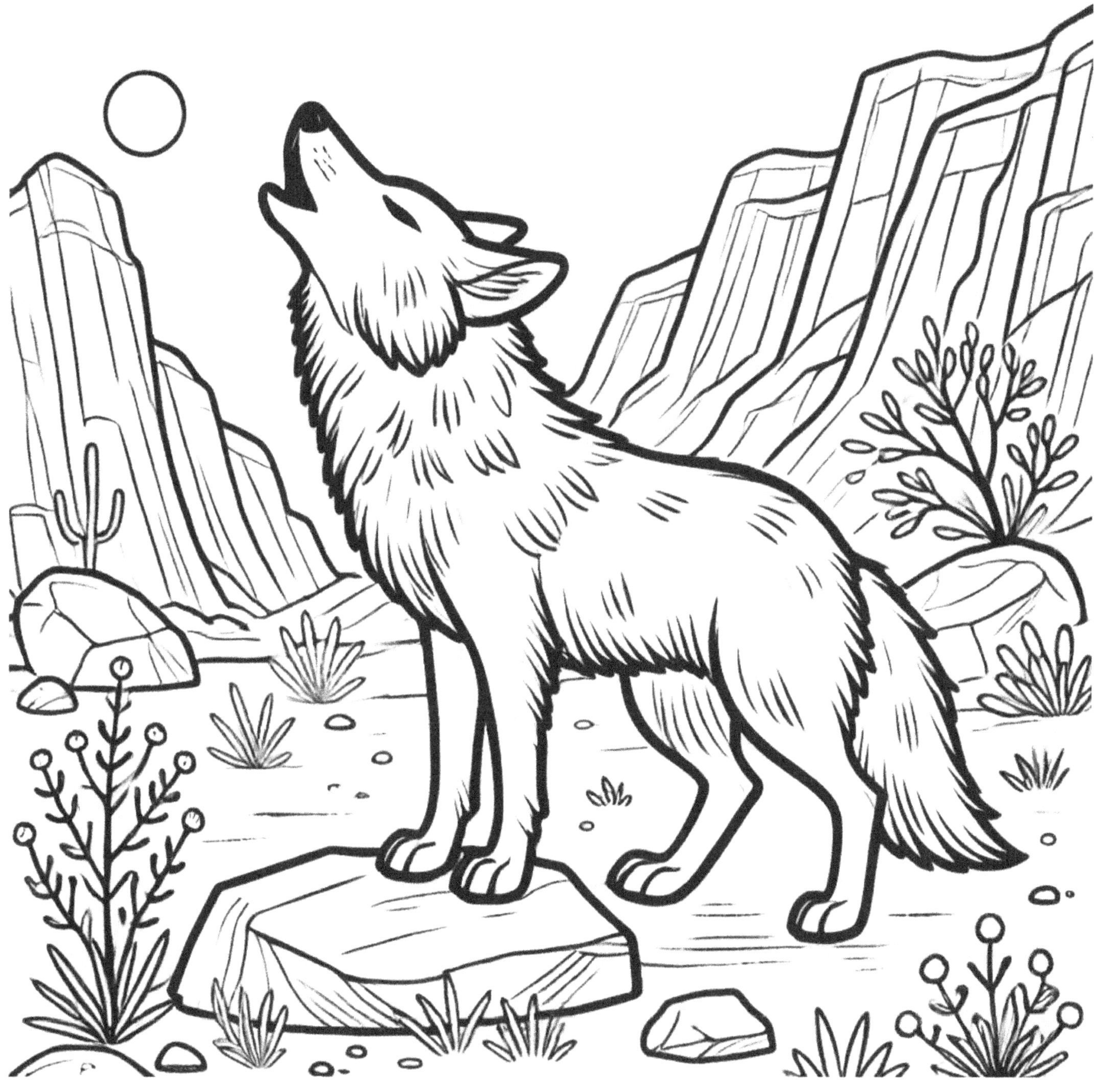

The state insect of Arizona is the beautiful two-tailed swallowtail butterfly. These butterflies are big and yellow with black stripes. You can see them fluttering around flowers in the summertime.

Question:

Have you ever seen a butterfly up close? What colors did you see?

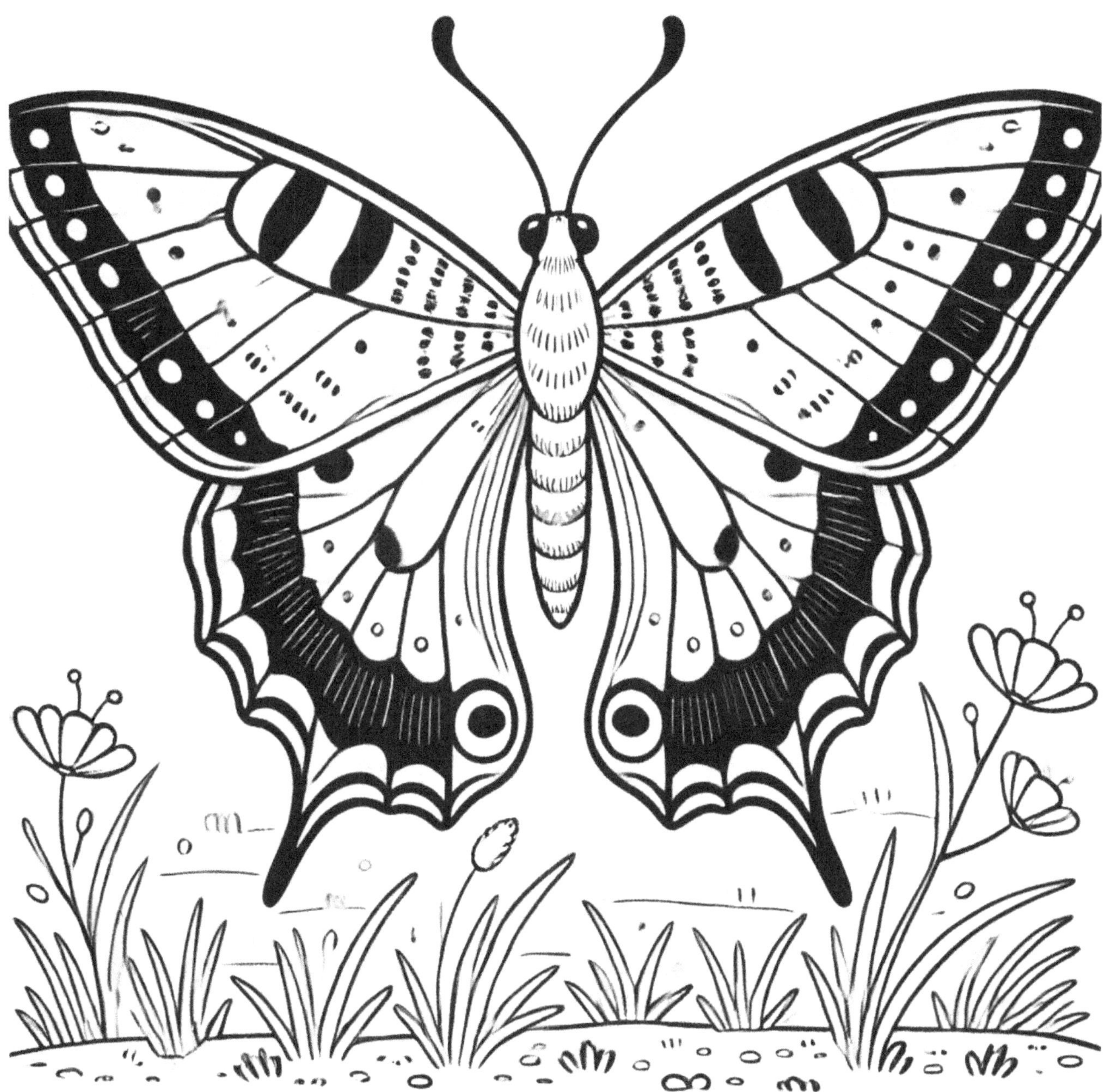

In Payson, you can learn about different kinds of snakes like the Arizona coral snake and the rattlesnake. Coral snakes are colorful with red, yellow, and black bands. Rattlesnakes have a rattle on their tails that makes a noise when they shake it.

Question:

Would you like to learn about different animals? What do you think snakes feel like to touch?

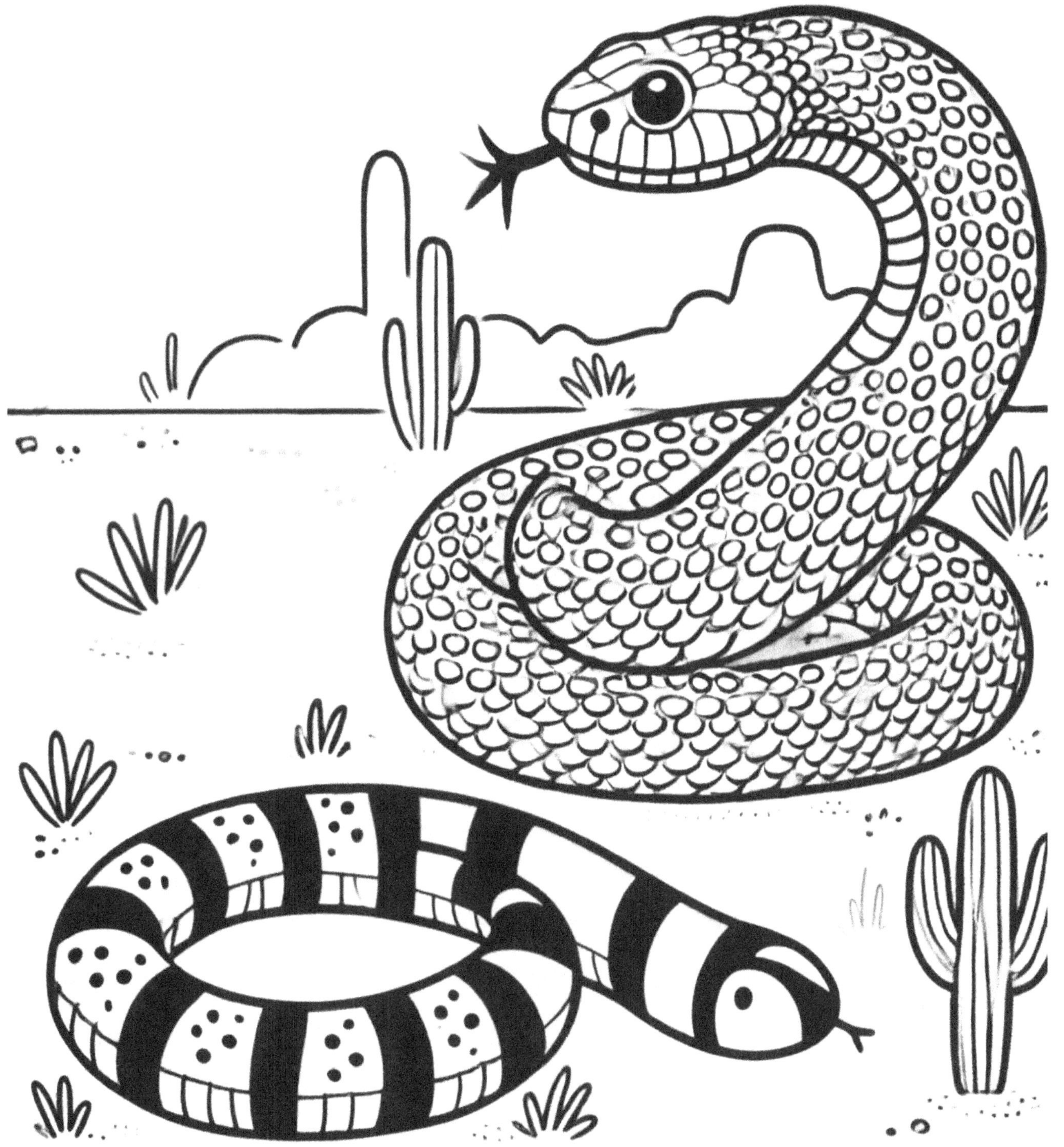

Payson is home to a variety of interesting insects. You can find colorful dragonflies flitting around ponds and streams, their wings shimmering in the sunlight. There are also busy bees, delicate butterflies, and many more fascinating creatures. Each insect has a unique role in nature, helping plants grow and keeping the environment healthy.

Question:

Do you like watching insects?

Which one do you think is the most interesting and why?

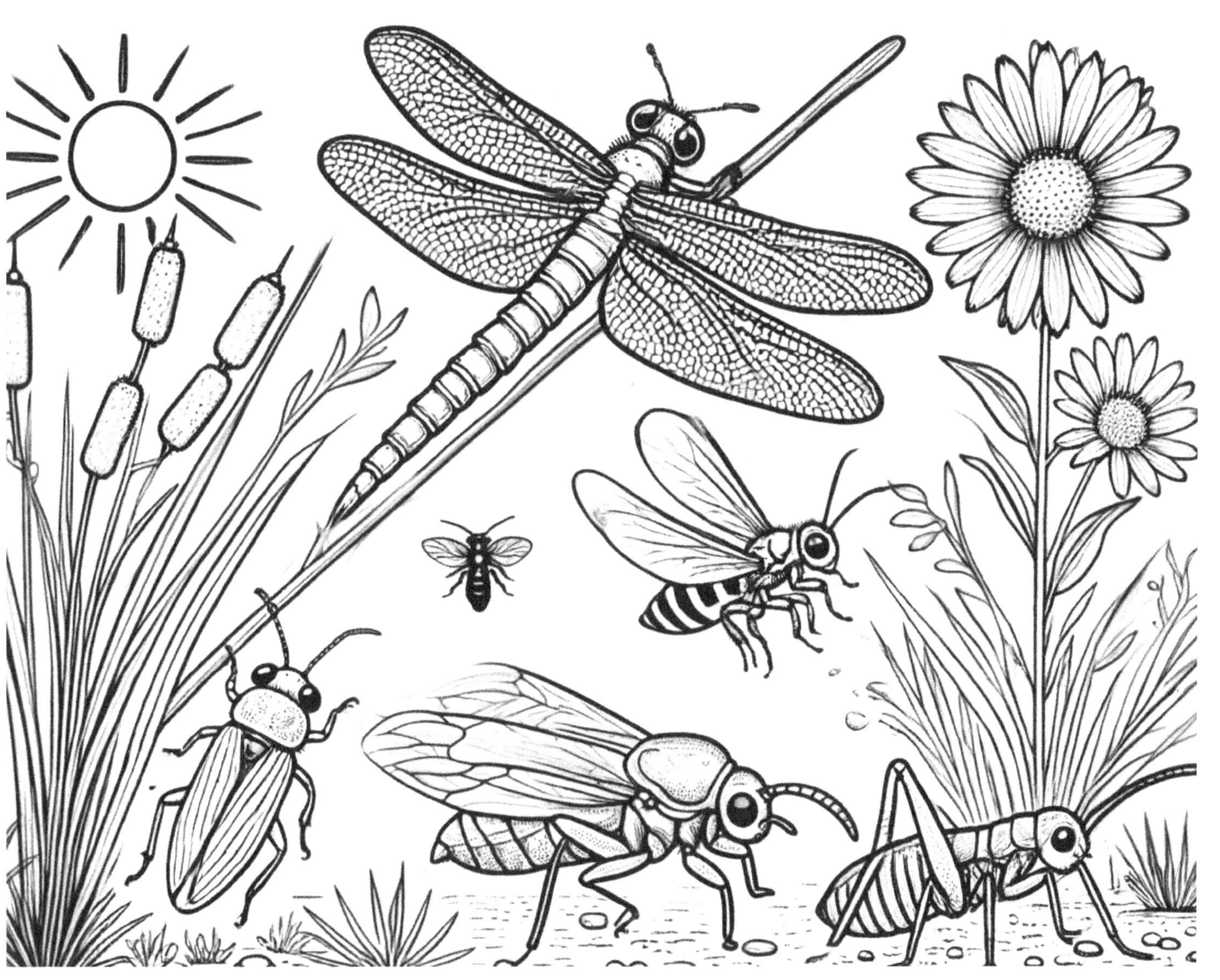

The prickly pear cactus is a unique plant that grows in the desert areas around Payson. It has flat, paddle-shaped pads covered in small spines. In the spring, the prickly pear blooms with beautiful yellow, pink, or red flowers. The cactus also produces sweet, red fruits called "tunas" that animals and people can eat. It's amazing how this cactus can thrive in the hot, dry desert!

Question:
Have you ever seen a cactus with colorful flowers? What color flower would you like to see on a prickly pear cactus?

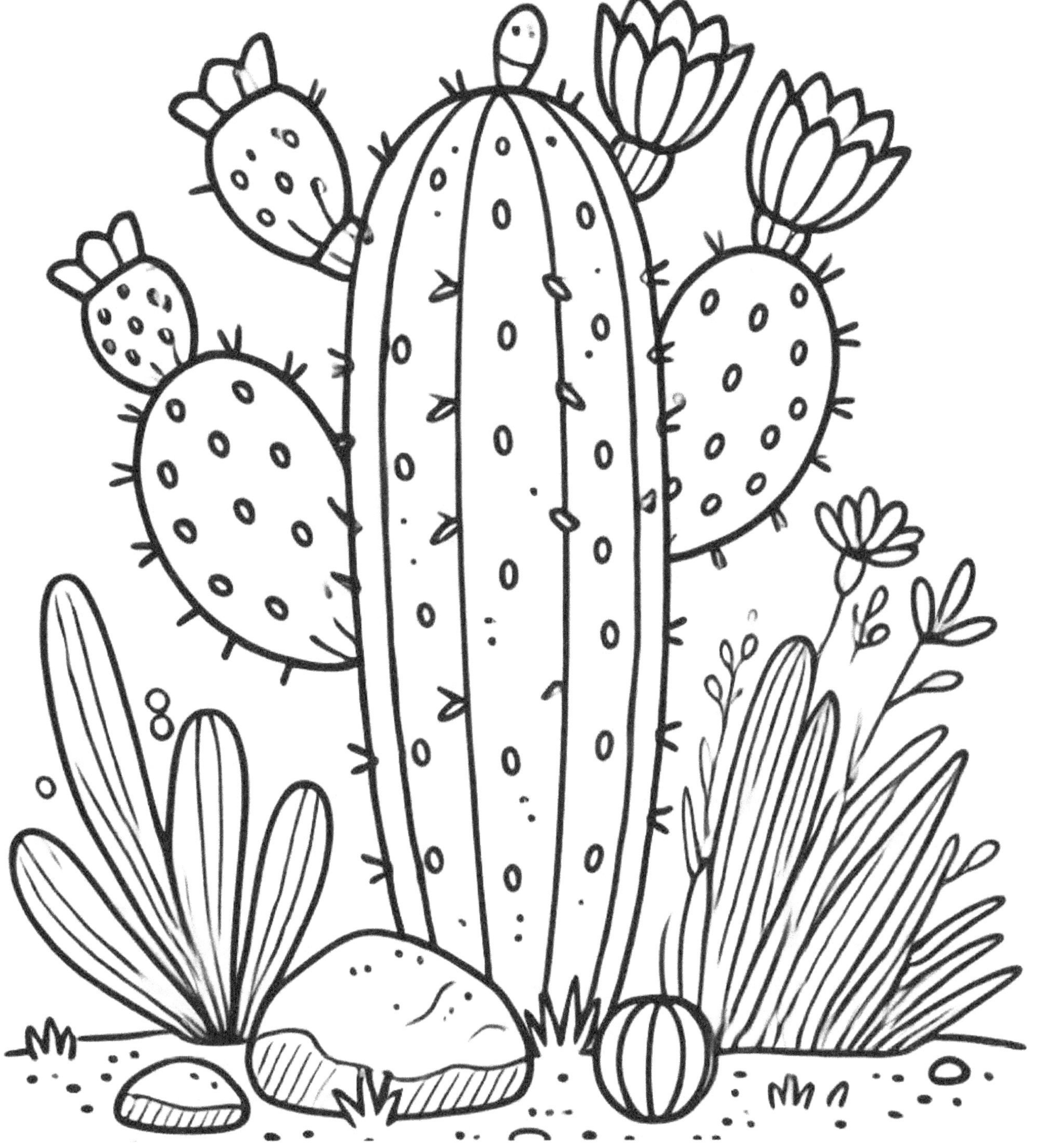

The Mogollon Rim is a beautiful, high cliff in Payson, Arizona. It stretches for miles and is covered with tall pine trees. From the top, you can see forests and valleys below. It's a great place to hike and enjoy nature.

Question:

Have you ever seen a place so high you can see for miles and miles?

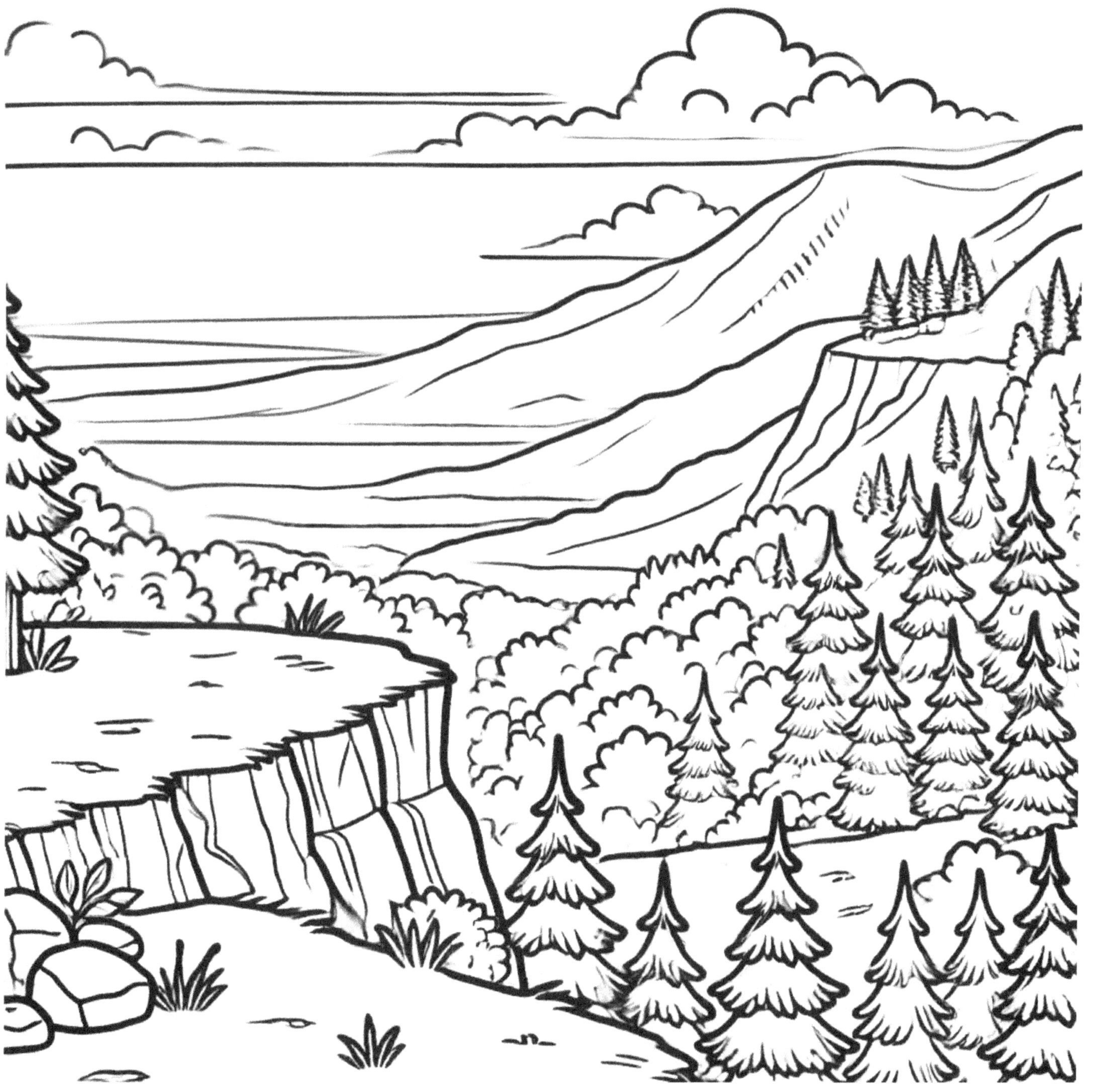

OK! Now you have seen some of the
beautiful places in Payson,
where do you want to go next?